S · A · P

*Inside the Secret
Software Power*

D1443207

S · A · P

Inside the Secret
Software Power

*SAP—die heimliche Software-Macht. Wie ein
mittelständisches Unternehmen den Weltmarkt eroberte*

GERD MEISSNER

McGraw-Hill

New York   San Francisco   Washington, D.C.   Auckland   Bogotá   Caracas
Lisbon   London   Madrid   Mexico City   Milan   Montreal   New Delhi
San Juan   Singapore   Sydney   Tokyo   Toronto

McGraw-Hill

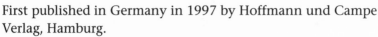

A Division of The **McGraw·Hill** Companies

First published in Germany in 1997 by Hoffmann und Campe
Verlag, Hamburg.
Title of the German original edition:
"SAP—die heimliche Software-Macht. Wie ein mittelständisches
Unternehmen den Weltmarkt eroberte"
Translated from the German by Jürgen Ulrich Lorenz

1 2 3 4 5 6 7 8 9 0   DOC/DOC   0 9 8 7 6 5 4 3 2 1 0

ISBN: 0-07-134785-2

This publication is designed to provide accurate and authoritative
information in regard to the subject matter covered. It is sold with the
understanding that the publisher is not engaged in rendering legal,
accounting, or other professional service. If legal advice or other
expert assistance is required, the services of a competent professional
person should be sought.
—From a declaration of principles jointly adopted by a committee
of the American Bar Association and a committee of publishers

 This book is printed on recycled, acid-free paper containing a
minimum of 50% recycled, de-inked fiber.

McGraw-Hill books are available at special quantity discounts to use as
premiums and sales promotions, or for use in corporate training programs. For more information, please write to the Director of Special
Sales, Professional Publishing, McGraw-Hill, 2 Penn Plaza, New York,
NY 10121. Or contact your local bookstore.

Contents

Preface to the U.S. Edition

When this book first hit the best-seller lists of leading German business publications, SAP reacted immediately, although predictably. Given the Germany-based public company's track record with journalists who dared to include less-than-flattering facts about the world's largest inter-enterprise software provider in their reporting, the furious letter from the corporate communications department came as no surprise.

The corporation had not prevented a wave of favorable reviews (by carefully playing down the book when asked for statements by the German business press). But the book about the world's fourth-largest independent software supplier had been critically acclaimed for all the wrong reasons, as the company's spokesperson Michael Pfister now felt compelled to point out in his official statement.

The mighty software giant, however, obviously did not find any factual fault with this account. SAP countered by referring to (unnamed) "callers from outside the company" who were quoted as saying, "This is not the SAP we know," ". . . distorted and not accurate," "The book doesn't get the picture of SAP" or "Topics with headline potential are overemphasized; some events and persons are given way too much importance."

The letter went on to accuse the author of "disqualifying Hasso Plattner [SAP's charismatic technologist and today's cochairman of its executive board] as a fan of fast cars and beautiful women." In short, readers should be warned: According to SAP's statement, this book is "over long stretches a piece of yellow journalism in book form."

Then again, that's probably the type of reaction a journalist has to live with when coming up with an independent account, not a PR brochure. SAP did not get to see the manuscript before publication and had no say in its outcome. To be fair, much to the surprise of fellow business journalists as well as of many SAP insiders, the company had decided to go along with the project anyway when its request for input was turned down. The author was given access even to sensitive (and sometimes less than flattering) information about the software giant to an unusual extent.

Judging the results will be left to the reader. At least Germany's most influential business and financial daily newspaper, *Handelsblatt,* not exactly a haven for sensationalism, was quite comfortable with the outcome. According to the paper, the book manages "based on properly researched facts and comprehensive conversations to inform a broad audience in a gripping narrative style about Germany's IT wonder company."

Any resulting wounds in Walldorf seemingly have healed since the book was first published in Germany in the fall of 1997. Hasso Plattner took the author on a personal tour of SAP's facilities in Palo Alto, Silicon Valley, in the spring of 1999. Plattner, one of the five original cofounders of the company, had just been joined at the helm of the company by Henning Kagermann, who replaced cofounder Dietmar Hopp. Today, Plattner and Kagermann share responsibility as co-chairmen of the executive board and CEOs of SAP.

Hopp and Klaus Tschira, the third remaining cofounder (out of five who started SAP in 1972), today serve on the company's supervisory board, Hopp as its still-very-active chairman. This book was researched and written in 1996–97. Since then, SAP has grown to more than 22,000 employees in more than fifty countries and has been listed (on August 3, 1998) under the symbol "SAP" on the New York Stock Exchange.

The transition of executive management from the founders to a new generation of managers whom the company had recruited directly from universities during the eighties (internally called the "Doktoren-Riege," which roughly translates to "Ph.D. Posse") went smoothly, much to the surprise of many analysts. This account can only give indications of how SAP—and all its Enterprise Resource Planning (ERP) software competitors—will cope with its biggest challenge yet: the Internet.

Other than the traditional SAP approach, which was based on a highly centralized software model, the new world of e-commerce allows for truly decentralized information processing and transactions. The company has reacted by starting its MySAP.com initiative in 1999, which provides an Internet portal (MySAP.com Marketplace) for industry-specific business communities and cross-industry collaborative solutions, now allowing individual users to customize their interface for specific business tasks.

It remains to be seen where that approach will lead the company. This, as well as describing the Internet's impact on the ERP business as a whole, would take another book.

For their valuable input and patient support with this one, I am especially indebted to my German editor, Hubertus Rabe, as well as to my wife, Andrea Klotz.

Gerd Meissner
Mountain View, California
December 1999

SAP—The Opportunity for Globalization

G rumbling is in, and the latest issue to grumble about is the so-called globalization trap. Workers' advocates complain of continuous wage concessions, longer working hours, and reduced social security benefits in a world economy tied together via computer networks. But this pessimistic view hides the opportunities the information society offers for individuals and businesses alike.

For more than twenty-seven years, SAP has been a significant force shaping the information society. The company has benefited Germany's Rhine-Neckar region, where its home office is located, and has created more than fourteen thousand new jobs. Its employee-owners receive top salaries and can take advantage of self-determined flextime. "SAP is not only a company, it is a job creation program," wrote Hamburg's *Manager Magazin.*

And SAP is a truly global company. "I can imagine some software projects that literally move around the world from east to west on a twenty-four-hour cycle, from person to person or from group to group, one working as the other sleeps," wrote Nicholas Negroponte, director of the Media Laboratory at the Massachusetts Institute of Technology, in his 1995 book *Being Digital.* This vision is reality at SAP. New software is developed in a process based on circulation—from Walldorf in Germany to Silicon Valley in California, Singapore, and Tokyo—coordinated by German headquarters.

If you ask people, "What is SAP?" you might get a shrug from some; others might answer, "Something to do with software." Why do even those interested in computers and software know almost nothing about the leading German software provider? It is true that sensational share price advances and a subsequent, no less spectacular tumble in stock price brought SAP AG to the front pages of many newspapers. But in contrast to Bill Gates, who set up Microsoft in 1975—three years after SAP was founded—almost nobody outside the software industry knows the names of the five high-tech pioneers (and now self-made multimillionaires) who founded SAP.

One possible reason is that the powerful software from Walldorf is discreetly running in the background at the offices of large and midsized companies, while the splashy Windows logo can be found on virtually every PC. Another is that the five founders of SAP set up their firm as a team and are less visible than a software star such as Bill Gates (except perhaps when one cofounder got out amidst much public conflict and sold his common shares, as Hans-Werner Hector did in 1996). A third reason could be that SAP remained a very "engineering-oriented company," as the *Financial Times* stated in 1993. And there's the fact that high-tech acronyms such as ALE (application link enabling), BAPI (business application programming interface), and ABAP/4 (SAP's programming language) do not necessarily catch the public's imagination.

Nevertheless, *Forbes* ranked SAP's CEO, Dietmar Hopp, with the power elite, one of the top ten most creative and successful persons in the world. Most multinationals—and, increasingly, midsized companies all around the world—are controlled by means of the standard enterprise software born in Walldorf. Bill Gates, a customer as well as a partner of SAP, uses SAP R/3 for financial accounting. So far, the SAP systems R/2 and R/3 have been a more important factor in the globalization of markets than the Internet.

Like IBM in the past, the software provider from Walldorf has been fiercely criticized. Usually SAP hit back roughly—sometimes justifiably, but not always so, as when SAP pulled advertisements from certain publications because of less than favorable coverage. "For SAP, dealing with criticism is not particularly easy," commented the German trade journal *Computer Zeitung* on the occasion of the twenty-fifth anniversary. But during the writing of this book (the suggestion for which came from outside SAP), the company's board members and employees received me kindly and spoke with remarkable openness. They also granted me access to confidential, delicate internal matters, which did not always cast the most flattering light on the company. Visits of several days (without PR "watchdogs") in the headquarters in Walldorf convinced me that "Openness as a management principle" is not just idle talk at SAP. Rather, that statement characterizes a progressive high-tech company with highly qualified and motivated employees who show a stronger commitment to their firm than employees at many other German companies. This book tries to explain why.

Structure of the Book

Part I of the book, "Development Phase, 1972–1980," describes the founding and early years of this remarkable company, which from the very beginning focused on real-time processing and the integration of application systems.

After starting with R/1, an accounting package, SAP developed the mainframe version of that package, R/2, which was the basis for SAP's growth in the 1980s.

Part II, "Products, Services, and Markets—Core Competencies," first discusses R/3, a real breakthrough product in enterprise software. How the package operates is illustrated by an account of an actual installation. The text then moves to the competitive situation, showing how the combination of a brilliant CEO, a customer-focused marketing strategy, and, last but not least, a unique product combined to make SAP a success in the United States. Finally, I turn to SAP's corporate culture, looking at it from the inside.

"Publicity," the third part of the book, deals with SAP's relations with the press, its stockholders, and the general public. Despite the company's impressive performance, which pleased its shareholders, SAP's media relations have been at times abysmal. Too, the conflict among the five cofounders that led to the resignation of one of them also received a large amount of publicity.

Part IV, "Outlook on the Future," discusses this software giant's ongoing activities, including its cooperation with Microsoft, its enhancement of R/3 with Internet and intranet functionality, and the clear advantage of R/3, with its use of four digits for years, in a Y2K-shaken world.

The "paradox of a book" was the phrase Nicholas Negroponte used to characterize authors' attempts to describe the fast-changing world of bits and bytes in this antiquated form. But if this book helps even those who do not know the first thing about computers to understand a little bit about the "adventure of SAP," it will have served its purpose.

The October 1996 Plunge of SAP's Stock

There is an enormous pressure to be successful.
—DIETMAR HOPP, COFOUNDER AND
CHAIRMAN OF THE ADVISORY BOARD, SAP AG

When Dietmar Hopp, age fifty-six, woke up on the morning of October 23, 1996, he had just lost $652 million.

Hopp, together with his family and the Dietmar Hopp Foundation (which he established), is the most important individual shareholder of the software giant SAP AG, the company characterized by a German business weekly as "a sort of Germanic Microsoft."

But on a Wednesday in the fall of 1996, at the stock exchange in Frankfurt and correspondingly on the PC screens in Walldorf, it looked more like Valhalla. The world market leader for enterprise software had just lost about one-fourth of its market capitalization— some $4.7 billion. Only one day before, SAP shares had traded at a higher price than BMW's, the favorite of the German stock exchange. As the market opened on this day, however, a frenzy of sell orders hit the Frankfurt stock exchange, and it took twenty-five minutes before the first quotation for SAP could even be fixed.

When the sell-off was over, SAP stock had plunged by $43.33, to $141.33.

"Sometimes I wished I weren't CEO of SAP AG," said Hopp after it was all over. Nevertheless, he added: "But so many positive things have happened to me because of SAP, so I thought: You have to get through."

It was because of this plunge of the stock price that the general public heard for the first time about SAP. They might have read in the newspaper that the company was founded in 1972 by five former IBM system engineers—Dietmar Hopp, Hans-Werner Hector, Hasso Plattner, Klaus Tschira, and Claus Wellenreuther—and that the acronym SAP stands for Systeme, Anwendungen, Produkte in der Datenverarbeitung (in English, Systems, Applications, Products in Data Processing). The company's success had been built on SAP R/2 and SAP R/3, enterprise software packages that handled financial and fixed-asset accounting, materials and logistics management, and human resources management in companies worldwide. Multinationals such as DuPont, Hoechst, Deutsche Bank, Coca-Cola, Deutsche Telekom, and even Microsoft use SAP software. Ninety-five of the top one hundred German companies rely on SAP's products, which are tailored to their needs by highly specialized consultants.

SAP, which had been started by five IBM dropouts, had developed into a multibillion-dollar business with more than twelve thousand employees. It achieved considerable stock price gains for its shareholders—"almost as reliable as a Swiss watch," cofounder Hasso Plattner boasted at one point.

But on that day in October 1996, SAP's own success was the company's undoing. The collapse of the stock price was caused by a briefing in which Henning Kagermann, a member of the SAP board, informed analysts of a revision in the latest forecast of company earnings: Based on the results of the third quarter, Kagermann explained, SAP had to revise its forecast for the fiscal year downward. Contrary to previous forecasts, it now seemed unlikely that SAP AG would be able to increase its profit before tax by more than 40 percent. Then Kagermann cautiously corrected himself downward—the company would try its best to achieve the 40 percent mark.

If other German companies had been able to announce such a profit increase, the stock exchange would have been happy. But a few months earlier, in July 1996, CEO Hopp had helped get investors in the proper mood for continued growth by announcing: "For 1996, we expect a sales growth of 40 percent and an increase of profit before tax of more than 40 percent." Now Kagermann had to inform United States analysts and others in a telephone conference that this goal would not be achieved.

"We recognized that a visible downward adjustment of the share price would be inevitable [because of this revised forecast]", remembers Hopp. But the extent of the price drop was surprising. At 6:30 in the evening after the sell-off, the CEO was sitting at his PC, where price quotations and sales figures could be retrieved with just a mouse click. He was beside himself. "This is incredible. It bowls me over," groaned Hopp. Four million preferred shares of SAP—10 percent of the total volume—had been traded on that day. The CEO's dry comment summing up the events of the day: "Indeed, that was a big mess."

Later, the CEO of the software provider that was ranked number 5 worldwide acknowledged that he himself probably caused this development with his forecast in the spring of 1996. The German business weekly *Wirtschaftswoche* commented, "Dietmar Hopp did not learn from his excessive optimism of the past," and Hopp admitted that they were right. At that moment he could not guess that, in the end, his forecast for the fiscal year would turn out to be right after all.

With a painful smile, the SAP boss remembers a headline in the *Münchner Abendzeitung.* "This Man Lost $652 Million Overnight," announced the newspaper on its front page. The paper also ran an article about SAP's troubles along with a not at all flattering color photo of Hopp. The image showed the always bolt-upright SAP boss—whose movements have been described even by longtime confidants as clumsy—looking the picture of misery in his custom-made suit: drawn-up shoulders, cast-down expression, worried frown. "My wife said, 'You poor sod,'" Hopp comments. "But I didn't overreact," adds the SAP boss quickly—which he might well have done, given his problematic relationship with the press.

"Is SAP badly off?" asked the weekly *Die Zeit* after the stock's plunge. The paper answered its own question at once: "Not at all!" And in fact only nine months later, in July 1997, the stock jumped to more than one and a half times its pre-plunge level, selling at $240.22.

The irony of company history was that it took an event like this—and the negative headlines that went with it—for SAP to be noticed and recognized as the world market leader in enterprise software.

Before the spectacular stock price drop, only stock exchange specialists and information-technology professionals had been interested in the software giant from Walldorf, about an hour's drive south of Frankfurt. But at that time, SAP had already existed for twenty-five years. It started on a Saturday in the spring of 1972—not in a garage, as with Silicon Valley companies like Hewlett–Packard, but in the narrow living room of an inconspicuous row house on the outskirts of Walldorf.

Part I

Development Phase, 1972–1980

Chapter One

Start-up—Leaving IBM's Open-Plan Office

We five cofounders of SAP worked in the IBM branch office in Mannheim. As everybody knows, the work climate in small units is often formed by the persons working together. So it was with us. There was only a flat hierarchy. We adopted and maintained this concept at SAP, too.

—DIETMAR HOPP

Years ago, anyone who wanted to make a mark in life was forced to leave Walldorf. "The misery was many-sided and big," said one chronicle of Walldorf in the eighteenth century. In those days, some two hundred families lived in "the village between the forests" on the edge of the Rhine plain, ten miles south of Heidelberg in Germany.

Despotic sovereigns, crop failures, and natural disasters caused the villagers to leave in droves. One of those to emigrate in 1783 was a young man, the last of four brothers, by the name of Johann Jakob Astor.

Starting out in New York first as a furrier, then working as a merchant and land jobber, this son of an alcoholic butcher from Walldorf changed the spelling of his name slightly, to John Jacob Astor, and soon became the richest man in America.

Historians and biographers may debate how to characterize Astor—was he a daring self-made tycoon, an unscrupulous exploiter and profiteer, or a generous philanthropist?—but Walldorf has fond memories of their great son, no doubt partly influenced by the donation of $50,000 left to the town in his will. With his legacy, a home for endangered young persons and the poor was built by the Astor Foundation and became the landmark of Walldorf, a town of fourteen thousand that is one of the wealthiest municipalities in the German federal state of Baden-Württemberg.

Now there is a video about the town designed to introduce visitors from the north of Germany, China, or the United States to the cozy town and the mysteries of the local dialect (called "Walderferisch babble"). As the video continues, the camera zooms in on the town's latest landmark, a six-story high-tech building that looms up gray and huge from the cornfields east of the Frankfurt-Basel autobahn, like the headquarters of an extraterrestrial insurance company that was plunked down there suddenly one night. Visible at quite a distance, the new—unofficial—coat of arms of Walldorf is formed by the three capital letters SAP, glowing in white neon like a beacon.

The people from Walldorf know very well to whom they are indebted for their newfound wealth. Consequently, the video does without a greeting by the mayor (and the chairman of the Astor Foundation). Instead, SAP cofounder Dietmar Hopp praises the location: "SAP, with its headquarters in Walldorf, has become a company with a worldwide reputation."

Meanwhile, the local newspaper attaches equal importance to the name of the SAP cofounder as to that of the other Walldorfer who, with slyness and cosmopolitan business sense, accumulated a gigantic fortune: "The Dietmar Hopp Foundation finances the construction of new apartments for senior citizens in Walldorf," rejoiced the local newspaper, published in Heidelberg.

But the bulging purse of the municipality of Walldorf is not due only to the software company. SAP settled in Walldorf in 1977, but by then an industrial area of 210 acres had been developed on the southern outskirts of Walldorf, on the border with the neighboring town of Wiesloch, and seventy companies had already set up shop there. Many of these enterprises are metal-processing companies. One of the biggest taxpayers, for example, is Heidelberger Druckmaschinen AG, the world market leader in printing machines. "Due to its stable economic structure, Walldorf can venture confidently toward the year 2000," summed up a town chronicle in 1970.

The First Steps

On a sunny morning in May 1972, not one of the young men who met in the narrow hallway of the row house on Odenwald Street was looking ahead as far as the year 2000. Only a stone's throw away from Astor House, within sight of the industrial area, this new housing development in Walldorf was primarily home to young, high-income families with children—like the family of Dietmar and Anneliese Hopp.

Until March 1972, the lanky engineer had worked for IBM as a system engineer in the branch office of the computer giant in Mannheim, half an hour's drive from Walldorf. On this warm Saturday, however, the dark green leather couch in Hopp's house served as the personnel office of his new firm. The young father with the boyish face had just set up a company with four ex–IBM colleagues in order to develop and sell computer software.

All along the quiet street, neighbors did yard work or polished the status symbols of the late years of Germany's economic miracle: angular BMWs, plump Opels, shining Audis. On the back terrace, Anneliese Hopp changed the diapers of her son Oliver, who had been born in April. His loud crying came through the open window of the living room. One might think a young father would not take the risk of leaving a secure career at IBM—but Hopp had other plans in mind.

Digression: Data Processing in the 1970s

The headquarters of IBM Germany are located in Stuttgart, the capital city of Baden-Württemberg. In the conservative southwest of Germany, Big Blue promised a good career, without surprises.

In 1972 most Germans were not particularly familiar with computers. As far as IBM was concerned, it was more likely that the IBM typewriter came to mind. In those days, *computer* was a synonym for *mainframe*—IBM 360s, which had a main memory of just 512 KB—a fraction of what is found in today's average PC. Often punch cards were still used to store data.

At IBM in Mannheim, Dietmar Hopp was regarded as an expert in what was called *dialog programming*. At the time, programmers' instructions were usually processed at night, when the computer had finished its normal daytime operations. But in dialog programming, the programmer caused the machine to process the programming instructions directly after input. This is how contemporary PCs work, and it seems self-evident now. In those days, however, it required a high level of technical expertise; the plus side was that it could substantially accelerate the developing and testing of software. "That's something he marketed like a genius," says a former IBM colleague of Hopp.

While in the United States at least eighty thousand computers were in use in 1972, in Germany only eight thousand computer systems were installed at the time. The huge equipment hummed in air-conditioned computer rooms. Tending these voluminous electronic giants, data processing professionals sat at consoles that reminded one of the control panels at power-generating stations. Most of these machines had been built by IBM, which dominated the market and had just introduced its latest model, the 370.

In the 1960s, most applications software—that is, computer programs for things like payroll accounting—was developed by the data processing departments of computer-using firms. Some was distrib-

6

uted by IBM with its computer systems, and for a long time IBM did not charge separately for its software. Such programs were regarded as an incentive to encourage companies to buy IBM's computers. But in June 1969 IBM had to stop bundling computers, system engineering services, customer training, and software in the face of a threatened antitrust suit.

Unnoticed by the public, a market niche thus emerged: the software industry. In 1972 only two dozen software providers were active in Germany. "Due to the PC, nowadays most people know what software is," says Dietmar Hopp. "In those days, only insiders were familiar with this technical term."

Taking the Risk

"I always said I would go out on my own," remembers Hopp. But his family and friends could not understand why the young father, having spent only four years with IBM, would choose an uncertain future with a product that still had a small market. "My in-laws weren't enthusiastic," recalls the SAP cofounder. "They were very anxious."

But Hopp, though an enthusiastic soccer player, was no gambler. In retrospect, he calls his decision to start his own company a "calculated risk."

"The people from Baden are generally regarded as particularly risk-averse, more so than the rest of Germany. This attitude is accompanied by a certain hostility toward technology. But I'm not a typical Badener. I was always willing to take risks," explains Hopp, who was born in the small village of Hoffenheim, located in a region called Kraichgau.

That morning in May 1972, Hopp and cofounder Klaus Tschira had invited two very promising programmers who had already attracted their attention during their time with IBM. To both new entrepreneurs the programming seemed to be "capable and enterprising enough," to use Tschira's words, and both were willing to give up their secure jobs for a new start in the fledgling software firm.

However, there was a problem. Both programmers worked for IBM clients that had been served by Hopp and Tschira—the tractor manufacturer John Deere, in Mannheim, and Pfaudler-Werke, a manufacturer of containers and apparatus in Schwetzingen. "Hiring these two programmers was pirating," admits Tschira. And the new firm could not offer its prospective employees much more than an idea and a few reasonable-sounding plans. "It would not have been responsible to make promises to them we couldn't be sure we could keep," says Hopp.

"In the beginning, I would never have believed that we would be so successful," Hopp told the newsmagazine *Der Spiegel* in 1995, twenty-three years later. Instead of great visions, the living room was buzzing with technical terms from business administration and information technology as the four talked shop: about "updating of master data" and "dialog programming," of "routines," "macros," and "data pools."

With a beer in his hand, Hopp explained to the visitors the simple concept the business of the new firm was based on. Whether in accounting or materials and logistics management, all IBM clients faced similar or even the same problems in developing their application programs. And each user had to reinvent the wheel, spending enormous sums for external consultants. Hopp and Tschira intended to exploit this opportunity, developing standard software that could be used by many companies. "From the very beginning, our concept was to set standards in information technology," emphasizes Hopp.

As the two programmers listened to Hopp, they had only one—albeit important—question: Where would the new entrepreneurs get a computer? Only industrial giants, banks, insurance companies, mail-order firms, or research institutes could afford such expensive monsters in 1972, and both programmers realized that computer equipment would be well beyond the means of a start-up company.

Hopp's answer cheered them. The new firm already had a well-known first client: the nylon fiber works of the British chemical giant International Chemical Industries (ICI). This customer was based in Östringen, a small town some six miles from Walldorf. ICI had agreed to let the newly established firm use its own computer to develop the software they wanted: an integrated software package for financial accounting, materials and logistics management, and order processing. The plan of the software experts was to sell the application system later as standard software to other customers.

Not until 1980, eight years later, did the company get a computer of its own. But in those first months things were especially tight, and in order to cover the day-to-day costs for their new business the founders even emptied out their savings accounts. "Our assets were really our people," says Hopp.

Cofounder Claus Wellenreuther

Claus Wellenreuther was a strange character in the open-plan office of IBM in Mannheim, where Big Blue resided in an office building opposite the main railway station. The gaunt MBA kept his thin blond hair rather long and loved wearing richly colored jackets and loud shirts—without a necktie.

In 1971 things were not nearly as stiff in the IBM branch office in Mannheim as in the headquarters of the electronics giant in Armonk, New York. There it was compulsory to wear a "uniform" of dark blue suit, white shirt, and tie. The nickname "Big Blue" comes not only from the firm's blue logo but also from those dark blue suits of its powerful army of system engineers and managers. Later, Bill Gates would call them "The Suits."

Nevertheless, at least a gray suit was also necessary at IBM in Mannheim in the early 1970s. But Wellenreuther cared as little about the dress code as he did about the unspoken requirement that IBM employees drive stolid, conservative, middle-class cars—"especially not sports cars," as a former colleague of Wellenreuther remembers. Old IBM soldiers frowningly took note as Wellenreuther drove up not in a neutral Opel, Audi, or Ford, but in a flashy Porsche.

Even now, the restless Wellenreuther contrasts quite startlingly with the less flamboyant Hopp. But already in 1972 the two made a better team than first impressions would suggest. "Wellenreuther and I were the main initiators of the new business," says Hopp.

After studying at the university in Mannheim, Claus Wellenreuther started his career with IBM in 1966 as a systems engineer. At that time, the company primarily recruited physicists, mathematicians, and engineers. "As an MBA, I was already considered exotic," chuckles Wellenreuther. But it turned out that his education in business administration was an advantage. He was regarded as a pioneer in a special field in which a growing circle of IBM clients was interested: software for financial accounting. Years after he left IBM, the bookkeeping software for IBM computers that he developed was still called the "Wellenreuther bookkeeping system." Hopp says, "*Bookkeeping* and *Wellenreuther* were used as synonyms."

Nevertheless, Wellenreuther had no illusions about his chances of making a career at IBM. IBM habitually left the development and implementation of application software to its customers. Application software professionals were regarded as a new species. Therefore, they had almost no chance to get to the top.

Explains Hopp, "At that time, IBM focused exclusively on hardware—software was regarded as 'lining and trimming' to make the hardware more attractive. That's how they looked at Wellenreuther's bookkeeping system, too."

In 1971 the freethinking sports car driver felt he had hit a dead end at IBM. The company had decided to centralize the development of accounting software, and Wellenreuther says, "I expected to be appointed as project manager because I had developed and implemented financial accounting systems all the time." For months he had crisscrossed Germany giving lectures and training courses to improve the image of the computer giant as a customer-oriented company. But that summer management decided that the software professional—who meanwhile had gotten a doctorate— was not suitable for a career as a senior IBM manager, and the accounting software project would be given to someone else to run.

"That was frustrating," he recalls. "I had to think about what the future had in store for me."

Wellenreuther took two months off in order to plan his next move. When he returned from his pause for reflection, Wellenreuther quit his job at IBM. On October 1, 1971, he set up his own systems analysis and program development business in his home in Weinheim, north of Heidelberg.

Wellenreuther's withdrawal caused considerable disturbances in the open-plan IBM office in Mannheim. Even after twenty-five years, one can get a sense from former colleagues' comments how the work climate deteriorated after he left. Quite a few software professionals on the seventh and eighth floors shared his "disappointment about the personnel policy," as Wellenreuther diplomatically puts it nowadays. Wellenreuther was popular, admired by his coworkers for his success at getting his doctorate while still working at IBM—he even discussed his dissertation, a sophisticated mathematical treatise on optimization, with fellow employees at lunch—and others took his departure as a sign to leave themselves. "The consequence was a mass exodus," states one of his former colleagues.

Among those who were influenced by Wellenreuther's decision to leave were two younger colleagues named Dietmar Hopp and Hasso Plattner. Wellenreuther was on the right track, they felt, and when Hopp and Plattner decided to leave IBM, Hans-Werner Hector and Klaus Tschira said that they would go, too.

Cofounder Hasso Plattner

Wellenreuther's first visitor after he established his new business in Weinheim was a former colleague from the IBM Mannheim branch with whom he had worked closely. Both were computer experts with a deep appreciation of the fine arts, and they shared a liking for fast cars and beautiful women. The name of the visitor was Hasso Plattner.

Born in 1944, Plattner was, like Wellenreuther, the type of bachelor the typical conservative German IBM manager would never trust with his daughter. At first sight, the active engineer with the piercing eyes whose dark curly hair did not stop at his shirt collar looked like the contemporary cliché of a rebellious student looking for pleasure. Such young people were seen not only in Berlin and Hamburg but also at the university and in public places in Heidelberg, to the horror of the diligent and honest Badeners.

But the charming physician's son with the roguish face didn't have a great deal in common with these people of the '68 generation—aside from his preference for hard rock, his creative restlessness, and a certain impulsiveness that later was proverbial at SAP, where a grinning Plattner, as deputy CEO, posed for the annual report's group photo of the board members as the only one with an open shirt collar and no tie.

The nonconformist Plattner joined IBM in 1968. After studying telecommunications at the university in Karlsruhe, Plattner interviewed for a job with Siemens. Years later the SAP cofounder recalled this interview for the *Wall Street Journal:* He knew right during the interview that he could never be able to work for Siemens. To Plattner it was like the post office.

But the decision to turn Siemens down was not easy for him, confesses Plattner now. Siemens offered the young electronics specialist a chance to work on the Spectra 47, a new computer with a state-of-the-art operating system. Siemens stood for development. Really, that was what he was looking for—something much closer to the technology, explained the engineer. Today, the father of the SAP software R/3 says with certainty that with Siemens he would have learned much more technically than he did with IBM.

Looking back, the software expert explains his start at IBM as an "emotional decision." "IBM *was* the field of business data processing. And I had an inspiration: To commercialize is better than to specialize."

At IBM, Plattner was regarded as a teleprocessing expert. Like dialog programming, in 1971 teleprocessing was still in its infancy. By means of this technology, data from distant locations were transmitted via telephone lines into the math computer and then processed. But in 1972 the cost of a terminal (that is, a visual display unit) was more than $7,800.

At IBM, Plattner was also regarded as a master of his trade. Both his superiors and his peers appreciated his analytic keenness and his technical creativity as well as his rousing personality and powers of persuasion. These qualities made him popular with IBM's clients, too. But sometimes Plattner could get carried away: "It is no secret that Plattner speaks better than he listens," ironically comments one SAP cofounder.

IBM assigned Plattner to work with Dietmar Hopp on implementing an order processing system on the IBM computer system in the ICI fiber works in Östringen. "There, Plattner really deserved all the credit," comments Hopp. The two of them developed the system so quickly that the enthusiastic ICI managers planned to place a follow-up order for a materials and logistics management system that could be integrated into the already finished order processing system. (This was the software that ICI would later hire SAP to come up with.)

The problem was that IBM was not willing to attach its systems engineers to one client for a longer follow-up project. The company had other plans, as the duo found out soon after Wellenreuther left. Hopp and Plattner were assigned to work as traveling software experts, whose know-how would be spread among many different customers.

The two system engineers had already discussed how application software could be composed of prefabricated modules, according to a building-block concept. In the follow-up order from ICI they saw the opportunity to develop an additional standard module for such a model and to increase their knowledge about business applications.

The demand for such standard application software was continuously increasing, as Hopp and Plattner knew from their discussions with customers. The "unbundling" (that is, the separate pricing) of hardware and software by IBM would strongly influence the structure of the computer industry, and as Hopp and Plattner saw it, one of the newly established software providers might well exploit this opportunity.

"At IBM we had the feeling that we did not have the liberty to be successful with such a development," summarizes Hopp. So the two of them developed the idea of going into the software business for themselves. And they thought they could convince their former colleague Claus Wellenreuther to join them as a partner for accounting software. That was the reason for Plattner's visit to Weinheim. And Wellenreuther agreed to join the team.

Cofounder Klaus Tschira

Dietmar Hopp and Hasso Plattner decided that Klaus Tschira should be the fourth member of their team.

The stocky physicist with the thinning hair and the slightly chubby face also studied at the technical university in Karlsruhe. He joined IBM in 1966 as a systems engineer in the commercial field. His colleagues regarded Tschira as a "practical man for many things," says Hopp. He was also admired for his memory for figures, though his coworkers were afraid of his occasionally caustic irony.

Business administration had not been his strong point when he began working at IBM. "For me as a physicist, terms such as *debit* and *credit* at first were a cultural shock," remembers Tschira. At his interview the IBM managers urged him to begin his career as a data processing instructor. Tschira had tutored in mathematics while a university student; "I am quite good in teaching," he says. Instead, however, he took a position as a systems engineer. But he also prescribed for himself a crash course in business administration. "At that time, having an MBA was thought to be the shortest way to the top at IBM," remembers Tschira. "The rest of us in the open-plan office mostly were sales representatives at IBM—except for Claus Wellenreuther."

Tschira believed that the development of state-of-the-art application software was in good hands with professionals who had a scien-

14

tific education. "At IBM we had a feeling that people with a technical and scientific background could understand business problems better than people with MBAs could understand technical matters," Tschira explains. "Nowadays, of course, many MBAs study information science as well."

As systems engineer for IBM computers of the 360 series, Tschira primarily served three customers: the tractor manufacturer John Deere, the automotive supplier Freudenberg, and the builder and contractor Bilfinger + Berger in Mannheim. He also instructed data processing professionals from IBM clients in the programming language COBOL.

COBOL—Common Business Oriented Language—goes back to the 1950s and was accepted in the following decades worldwide as the standard programming language for commercial data processing. Remembering the COBOL classes he taught, Tschira says with a grin, "Never again did I learn so much in such a short time, because twenty participants made mistakes for me! You cannot make so many mistakes all alone."

For the project at John Deere, Tschira familiarized himself with the DOS operating system. This software, developed by IBM in the early 1960s, controlled the basic functions and peripheral units of the 360 system, allowing the machine to process several programs simultaneously. His know-how was useful when IBM introduced the considerably more efficient successor system OS. And when Dietmar Hopp, Hasso Plattner, and Claus Wellenreuther decided to go out on their own, they agreed that the planned standard software should be designed for the next generation of computers.

"Then Hopp started to look around for someone who could be a useful addition to the new team. And I was an expert at the conversion of application programs from DOS to OS," recounts Tschira, who is responsible for developing most of SAP's human resources management software. "So I signed on."

Cofounder Hans-Werner Hector

Hans-Werner Hector recalls that Dietmar Hopp asked him in a quiet corner of the open-plan office at IBM: "Would you like to join us? What we do at each IBM client is always the same. Therefore, it can be standardized."

The gaunt mathematician, who was born in 1940, studied at the university in Saarbrücken. He started with IBM in Mannheim in 1967, and was trained together with Claus Wellenreuther.

"My start at IBM was easy because I had several years' programming experience," says the fifth SAP cofounder. As a student he developed—still on a punch card system—software for an engineering office. "The Rhine bridge in Maxau is based on my programs."

At IBM the tall consultant with the prominent nose was assigned primarily to accounting systems. "When I finished my basic training, a sales representative grabbed me and said, 'Come with me.' He then introduced me to a client as a specialist in payroll accounting, and promptly excused himself," Hector says with a chuckle. "The problem was that I had never seen a payroll accounting system before."

As his SAP colleagues point out, Hector's special talent is learning by doing. So with the payroll department, he defined in detail what they needed and how they processed data.

In this way, Hector wound up working in Wellenreuther's domain, financial accounting. Hector was regarded as an expert in production planning systems, too, according to Dietmar Hopp.

In 1972 Hector was approached by Hopp and told that he, Plattner, Wellenreuther, and Tschira were starting their own firm. Hector liked the idea, "but I had to convince my wife that we wouldn't starve," remembers Hector with a smile.

The New Firm

With the last team member aboard, the five cofounders went to the office of the head of the IBM branch in Mannheim to inform him of their plans. His response was "How can you do such a thing?" Nevertheless, the five were firmly committed to the new enterprise, and on April 1, 1972, the new firm was established as a company constituted under German civil law. As the name of the firm they chose what Claus Wellenreuther had been using: System Analysis, Program Development. At first, Claus Wellenreuther's house in Weinheim served as their business address.

The first two SAP employees, Paul Neugart and Ulrich Daub—today SAP sales manager for Germany and head NCR alliance manager at SAP, respectively—quit their jobs in May 1972 and began working for SAP on October 1, 1972.

"My intention was to build a team that covered many aspects of enterprise business applications," summarizes Hopp, looking back. "This seemed to be the ideal team. We were on a first-name basis with each other and were friends right from the beginning—but not so close that we hung out together when we weren't working. That was good, because conflicts often arise on the private side.

"For twenty-four years we settled all our business conflicts—sometimes fiercely, but always fairly," he adds. "In the end, we always found a basis for an agreement, because everybody said, 'We can't let this fall apart.'"

Claus Wellenreuther, who left SAP in 1980 and now operates DCW Software in Mannheim, a company specializing in business applications, confirms this. "We never had quarrels—only clashes over methods."

"We really were a super team," concludes Hopp. However, the CEO of SAP AG could not help making an additional remark: "But our fifth cofounder was part of this, too, and obviously he found other advisers—I mean Hans-Werner Hector." However, the story of how Hector came to leave SAP on less than friendly terms must be reserved for a later chapter.

Chapter Two

Growth Phase—"We Learned with Each Implementation"

By working nights on borrowed computers, they won their first contracts. Twenty-three years and a lot of hard work later, they became Germany's first software billionaires.
—THE WALL STREET JOURNAL, APRIL 11, 1995

I n SAP's initial stages, the business secrets of the small firm could be stored on a few punch cards. Indeed, a batch of colored punch cards with writing on both front and back served Dietmar Hopp as mobile data storage. On his punch-card "laptop" the software entre- preneur wrote down important customer data and details about deals as well as notes on software development. For more than ten years the SAP boss relied on his "pasteboard planner," which was always in the inside pocket of his jacket; even after SAP established an office in Mannheim, the industrial center of the Rhine-Neckar region, and then in Walldorf, the young entrepreneur very rarely visited it.

Nowadays a company that operates the way SAP did in its early days would be called a "virtual enterprise." But in 1972 the five IBM dropouts and their employees were condemned to travel constantly because they could not afford a computer of their own and had to develop their software products in the data processing centers of their customers. "We could use their computer for free," Claus Wellenreuther says, laughing.

SAP established its first "development center" in ICI's synthetic fiber works on the outskirts of Östringen. This plant, established in 1965, had three thousand employees (later the factory was taken over by DuPont). On ICI's IBM computer the SAP people developed System R (later also called R/1), the archetype for what would become the market-dominating SAP software packages R/2 and R/3. At the end of the first fiscal year, there were nine employees on the payroll of SAP. The company achieved a sales revenue of $194,360 and even turned a small profit. According to several SAP employees back then, Hopp proclaimed, "We will never have more than thirty employees in order to ensure a manageable size."

The new financial accounting system, System RF (*RF* stands for "real-time financial accounting"), was finished in 1973 and became the cornerstone for SAP's success. In the same year SAP won two additional well-known companies as customers: the cigarette manufacturer Roth-Händle, in Lahr, and the pharmaceutical manufacturer Knoll, in Ludwigshafen. With these clients, too, SAP used their IBM mainframe computers to develop the software they requested.

In 1977, SAP transferred its office to Walldorf, where it rented space in an office building. Three years later, in 1980, the development phase was completed, and SAP was number seventeen on the list of the top twenty software providers in Germany. By the time the company moved into its own building in the industrial area of Walldorf, fifty of the top hundred German industrial enterprises were SAP customers—but that was only the beginning. "From 1980 on, it just went up," says the SAP chairman, looking back.

In 1982, ten years after the establishment of the firm, SAP's one hundred employees achieved a sales revenue of $10 million. The company had 250 customers, all large enterprises. And for the first time, SAP could cover all business applications with its new software package, R/2, which it had started developing in 1978. With R/2, for mainframes, and eventually R/3, for client-server computing, the midsized high-tech company rapidly—and almost unnoticed by the public—grew to a multinational group. "Hopp manages a firm that hardly anybody knows," wrote the newsmagazine *Der Spiegel* in 1994.

"It is a very engineering-oriented company," an analyst wrote in the *Financial Times*, trying to explain the SAP phenomenon. True to that image, for many years SAP relied on the reputation of its software and word-of-mouth referrals through managers and external consultants; only in 1986 did SAP exhibit at a computer show, and the company's first product and image advertisement didn't begin appearing in trade journals until 1988. "If something was not right, we responded immediately," recalls R/2 expert Jürgen Hachenberger. "All of us programmed, with Hopp and Plattner taking the lead. We knew that we were developing a unique product."

But what makes the SAP software unique? Standard software as such is no invention of SAP. Prefabricated business application software was offered in Germany as early as 1969 by ADV/Orga. In 1974 SAP made a distribution arrangement with ADV/Orga; however, it was canceled in 1980, and in the early 1990s this software provider was taken over by the Sema Group. Other firms such as MBP, a subsidiary of the steel mill Hoesch, and SCS, from Hamburg, offered standard software, too. The suspicion of the SAP founders that their idea "will be taken up by the big players as soon as it appears to be a success," as Dietmar Hopp put it, proved true. Plus, the R/2 system had to hold its own against fierce competition by the IBM systems IFS and Copics. Why, of all these software providers, did SAP succeed in getting its software accepted as the standard in information technology for enterprises of all sizes in all types of industry worldwide? That's a question that can be answered only by looking at how the company developed.

In 1976 SAP changed the legal form of its business into a limited-liability company: SAP GmbH—Systems, Applications, and Products in Data Processing. Four years after its founding, the company still had neither business premises for its twenty-five employees nor a computer of its own. The managing directors were Dietmar Hopp and Claus Wellenreuther. At that time, the former IBM systems engineers were already regarded as veterans in the software business—unlike the young computer tinkerers Paul Allen and Bill Gates, who had established Microsoft in April 1975.

In Mannheim, Claus Wellenreuther rented an apartment on the fourth floor of an old building, to be used as a secretary's office and a place to have a telephone. In its initial stages, the office equipment of this high-tech company was restricted to a Xerox copying machine, a few IBM Selectric typewriters, and some telephones.

The secretary was Anneliese Vogel, who in the first years held the flying squad of programmers together by telephone. Her rapid and flawless way of giving the firm's full name when she answered the telephone—"System Analysis and Program Development, hello"—soon earned her the nickname "System Anneliese." Only seldom did she catch sight of the SAP founders, who would occasionally drop by for meetings or for "coding" (programming).

In the initial years of the software industry, it was enough to have a desk to write at. For programmers, access to the computer was not necessary before the test phase, for all software was developed in writing. The instructions had to be written on specific "punch forms" that afterward, by means of card punches and verifying units, were transferred to punch cards that could be read by the computer.

Of the SAP founders, only Claus Wellenreuther had an office of his own in Mannheim. The expert for financial accounting software served as a "firm within the firm," so to speak, continuing to serve customers who used an accounting system that he had developed for IBM computers. Unlike the always correctly dressed Dietmar Hopp, the long-haired Wellenreuther didn't think twice about doing his customer visits and presentations in an open-necked silk shirt, linen trousers, and sandals. And customers never failed to be astonished the first time they saw Wellenreuther's strange ritual: Every time the tall SAP cofounder left a room after a meeting, he would jump up as he passed through the door, grab the top of the door frame with both hands, and hang there for a few seconds.

Digression: Batch and Real-Time Processing

When SAP started, batch processing dominated in data processing. Wellenreuther's software was a batch-oriented accounting system, too. That meant that the entries first had to be keyboarded by typists at special data acquisition equipment. Then they were stored, and afterward processed in batches in the data processing center at night or at certain specified times. The problem with this approach was that there was always a time lag between business activities and the processing of the corresponding data.

In batch processing with sequential data carriers, the data were stored on numbered magnetic tapes that had to be put in a magnetic tape drive one by one. Only then, long after data acquisition, could the data be processed by the computer.

With batch processing it was not possible to closely control relevant business processes. For example, before an incoming order could be processed and compared with available stock, the required materials might run critically short. Furthermore, batch processing was regarded as especially error-prone. Wrongly typed-in account or item numbers, for example, very often were detected only when the program run was already finished. Such input errors required expensive corrections afterward.

The solution lay in the *R* with which SAP marked its new software. It was a signal for information technology (IT) professionals that this software was designed for real-time data processing—that is, the data are processed immediately after input. What is taken for granted by PC users today was regarded as a revolutionary concept back then, because real-time processing used the scarce main memory of mainframe computers twice: once to process the data and a second time to control the visual display unit. "Over and over again we bumped into the technical limits of existing hardware and software," remembers Hasso Plattner.

At this time, United States research institutes were already exper-

22

imenting with a data network—later called the Internet—by which messages could be transmitted from computer to computer. But data processing professionals at United States or German companies still understood the word *teleprocessing* to refer to the technology that allowed the computer to communicate with a printer or a visual display unit via a cable. While the United States engineer Doug Engelbart had developed by 1970 a computer system that was controlled by means of function windows on a screen, and had previously presented in 1964 a tool for controlling the computer that he called a "mouse," hardly anybody took notice of these. The special computers on which such innovations could be tested, for the time being, were left to the United States Army, large-scale research institutes, or private high-tech centers such as Xerox Parc in California. In 1971, however, the small California electronics manufacturer Intel presented the first commercially available microprocessor, its model 4004—the ancestor of today's PC processors—beginning the process that would one day change the computer world in ways nobody could yet imagine. However, it would take an additional decade before the first IBM PC was introduced with an operating system that Big Blue licensed from Microsoft.

In the start-up phase of SAP, the traveling software professionals depended on the head of each data processing center and his team when they wanted to get hold of valuable running time for testing their programs on the mainframe of a customer. The best chances were at night and on weekends, when the computer had finished its planned batch runs. When the software developers—armed with packs of punch cards, lead pencils, and erasers—marched into their customers' data processing centers, they often brought a case of beer with them. This could considerably increase the data processing operators' readiness to help the SAP team. Once they began, they very often programmed straight through the night.

Under these circumstances, modern management was a sheer necessity at SAP. All the programmers were working toward the same goal, but sometimes they didn't really pay attention to how their efforts interacted with those of their colleagues. It was up to Dietmar Hopp to weld a bunch of very individualistic programmers, with different temperaments, into a team. "By then, Hopp's strong point—his ability to hold the staff together like a soccer team—revealed itself for the first time," recounts Plattner.

Every Friday afternoon, SAP's scattered employees met for their weekly staff meeting in the Pizzeria Venetia on the main street in Östringen. Over pizza and beer they discussed new coding and sales strategies. "The hard-and-fast rule was: At six o'clock we play soccer," remembered Hartmut Engel, the head of SAP Consulting. Out of this developed the firm's sports tradition—something for which young applicants often weren't prepared. "Among other criteria, I assess candidates by whether they participate in team sports," explains board member Gerhard Oswald.

Later on, SAP built extensive sports facilities into its Walldorf headquarters. Its employees now regularly compete in international soccer and tennis tournaments that are organized by the company. Chairman Hopp, however, still prefers golf (his handicap is 15) to soccer. "Usually, I'm accompanied on the golf course by people who are ready to bet on who will play best," says the SAP cofounder. In St. Leon-Roth, near Walldorf, where SAP operates a printing and shipping center, the multimillionaire established a private golf club that is also open to SAP employees and guests of the company. But the typical SAP employee's answer to the question of who or what they would like to be in another life would be pretty much like this one, given without hesitation by an employee who is a soccer fan: "Franz Beckenbauer."

Superiority of SAP Software

The young firm worked out a deal with its first client, ICI, to let SAP use ICI's computer to demonstrate their programs to prospective clients. Hopp was the one who met with potential customers. "He could best negotiate contracts and got out most for us," says Hans-Werner Hector, who praises Hopp for his "ability to think about winning rather than just about his pride. If someone had kicked me out of his office, I would not have visited him again—but that's certainly not good for business." At a company party once, the employees recited this ditty about Hopp: "If a customer kicks him out the front door, he'll come back in the back way."

ICI also let SAP have two rooms in the ICI building in Östringen. One they used as a secretarial office, which was so busy that the secretaries soon began answering the phones with "SAP" instead of the firm's full name. The second office primarily was used for coding. There, despite their limited resources, the cofounders developed several fundamental methods that were to set standards for all future business software.

They developed special programs that would allow the fiber works' IBM 360 to emulate the improved hardware performance of its successor, the IBM 370. This new computer, which the fiber works eventually installed, was planned to be the target platform for the sophisticated SAP software. On the IBM 2260 visual display units that were connected with the 360 computer, in turn, the technical possibilities of the powerful IBM 3270 visual display unit—which soon became the standard user terminal for IBM mainframes—were emulated. "It was a proven SAP principle that we did not limit ourselves to what existing computers were capable of. Rather, we banked on what future hardware would be able to do. This enabled us to develop attractive products," explains Dietmar Hopp.

SAP positioned its RF financial accounting software—its first standard software package—as a technically superior alternative to classic batch programs such as IFB from IBM. For the very first time, terminals were used as interactive workstations for real-time processing and dialog processing. Instead of the sequential processes of inputting data, storing it, and processing it later, real-time software made it possible to communicate directly with the computer. Thus, for example, accounting data could be checked for plausibility on the screen during input.

In order to use the scarce computer resources in an optimal way, the SAP pioneers divided their programs into dialog and database processes. For that purpose they designed dynpros, dynamic programs that controlled data exchange between computer and user by means of screen masks that could be adjusted flexibly to the relevant program. (Even today, with R/3 using up-to-date windows for this purpose, internal SAP usage still refers to them as "dynpros.")

The modern SAP programming language ABAP/4, by means of which R/3 modules can be developed on screen for various applications, originated in that room at ICI as well. The archetype of ABAP, developed by Klaus Tschira, was a report generator that bundled up specific query instructions (macros) that facilitated the analysis of company data according to defined criteria. But the highly sophisticated R/3 development tool ABAP/4, a powerful fourth-generation programming language, has only its name in common with this predecessor; ABAP/4, which SAP developers used for writing R/3 applications, is a highly sophisticated tool that makes R/3 the unique product it is.

SAP organized its software early on to conform to the *no-posting-without-voucher principle*, which is accepted as the standard in current business data processing. To comply with this accounting principle, it must be possible to trace back each individual bookkeeping operation. The approach developed by SAP stored all the data of each transaction as a unit in a database instead of storing each individual piece of information separately. Thus it could be ensured that the history of any voucher could be reconstructed and checked for plausibility with the press of a key.

However, real-time processing, dialog processing, and the no-posting-without-voucher principle were only means to an end. Right from the beginning, the uniqueness of SAP software consisted of radically integrating the different business information processes for the first time. "For us, real-time processing and integration were like brother and sister," explains SAP cofounder Tschira.

Until SAP came along, business data were analyzed in several batch runs or were not even processed electronically. Financial data, for example, were centrally collected and input by data typists. An accounting clerk had to wait for the batch run, when a pile of printer paper brought him up to date. But now SAP made it possible for the first time to combine the gathering and analysis of business data in one job.

In the past, business processes frequently had been divided among several departments. Thus the same data were collected in several different places—an inefficient system, to say the least. With the SAP software, they could be assembled by the computer into easy-to-grasp jobs that could be planned, controlled, and analyzed centrally. "The point was to make available a system that at any time could answer information requests," Klaus Tschira explains.

The basic idea of the pioneers was this: Important data should be collected only once—at the source. Why should suppliers' invoices be fed in entry by entry in the accounts payable department? Costs could be reduced by going back to the original order (provided that the order was electronically issued), because most of the data on an invoice already exists on the purchase order—purchase order number and quantities, for example. If the receipt of goods is handled electronically as well, then the checking and auditing of invoices can be automated.

Translating such ideas into computer programs was up to Hasso Plattner, because of his wealth of technical ideas and his ability to motivate people. "Of course, Plattner was the motor. He had the good ideas," said Paul Neugart, SAP's director of sales for Germany.

Already in 1973, the high degree of integration that is regarded as the strong point of the latest SAP software, R/3, was emphasized in an operating manual for the ICI accounting system: "Working areas that in conventional accounting had to be assigned to several employees or working groups can from now on be grouped logically, making staff reduction possible." Because of this potential for cuts in staff, the implementation of software with such far-reaching consequences made the trade unions step in—particularly in Germany. Frequently, implementation of SAP software has been treated as an issue that requires codetermination and specific plant agreements.

The fact that quite a few critics—particularly in the computer-phobic 1980s—exaggeratedly characterized SAP as a synonym for controlling employees and reducing the labor force may partly explain why SAP has long been cautious about presenting itself to the public. Dietmar Hopp addressed this issue at some length in his address on the twenty-fifth anniversary of SAP: "In most cases the implementation of SAP software did not reduce the labor force, but changed the structure of the jobs. While highly qualified jobs were added, the growth of less qualified jobs could be limited."

SAP also often met with stiff opposition among IT professionals at large enterprises who had been developing proprietary software up till now. These IT professionals saw standard software as jeopardizing their jobs. Some IT managers were afraid of losing their status as head of the in-house programming department. After all, the decision to switch to an external provider's software usually wasn't exactly a mark of confidence in the existing software and the people who developed it.

Computerwoche—A Critical Reviewer

The magazine *Computerwoche*, two years younger than SAP and for a long time the favorite publication of IT professionals in Germany, chronicled the rise of SAP from a midsized software provider to a worldwide company through two decades' worth of reports and comments—at times critical, often belligerent, never boring. In August 1977 *Computerwoche* editors Dieter Eckbauer and Elmar Elmauer interviewed both managing directors of SAP, Dietmar Hopp and Claus Wellenreuther. All persons involved remember the meeting in Munich with fairly mixed feelings.

Presswise, Dietmar Hopp went through a baptism of fire at this meeting. "Eckbauer was always a professional," concedes the SAP boss, and Claus Wellenreuther uses similar words. However, after this first meeting they felt as though they had walked into the journalists' trap, so to speak. In contrast, Dieter Eckbauer, editor in chief of *Computerwoche* from 1979 to 1995, comments: "SAP did not know the first thing at all about how to handle the press."

The reason for the anger of both SAP directors was that *Computerwoche* homed in on the sore point of SAP's corporate strategy: the company's dependence on the market-dominating computer giant IBM.

The success of SAP was actually based on a balancing act. On one hand, the young firm depended on IBM because its software was developed for IBM computers. Therefore, from the point of view of *Computerwoche*, SAP was only one of dozens of German software providers that followed the undisputed market leader into the data processing centers as loyal software vassals. And because they had begun at IBM, the SAP founders were regarded as typical IBM derivatives. "In the first fifteen years the company was absolutely uninteresting," says Dieter Eckbauer.

On the other hand, SAP had to hold its own against IBM as a competitor, first with the batch software IFB and then with the standard software IFS for IBM mainframe computers of the 370 series. *Computerwoche* journalistically benefited from this conflict in 1977 for the first time—and later over and over again.

The trade journal asked the SAP cofounders to compare both IBM programs—IFS had just been announced—with their own software. "We had just replaced an IFB accounting system and could give them fantastic figures," says Hopp. "Then *Computerwoche* assembled our statements in such a way that it made it look as if we were knocking IBM." Hopp and Wellenreuther did not feel happy about the meeting. Says Hopp, "We were afraid how IBM would respond."

This interview was published as the first installment in a two-decade-long series of reports on SAP in *Computerwoche*. Some of the magazine's reports were unflattering, as were some of SAP's responses: In 1995 the company responded to a bad review of R/3 with an advertising boycott.

However, often enough *Computerwoche* also positively or at least neutrally reported on SAP. A permanent conflict, as some observers suppose, cannot be inferred from such episodes. Even the interview in 1977 was really harmless, as Dietmar Hopp admitted after several years: "In all, the article made sense. It did not do any harm, as we feared—although we were prepared for the worst."

Standard Software

In the meeting with the *Computerwoche* editors, Hopp and Wellen-reuther did not yet talk about "standard software." In contrast, Hopp explained: "You must offer the user customized solutions." But this tactical statement was meant only to differentiate SAP software from the financial accounting software that was "fobbed off" (Wellenreuther's term) on IBM customers along with the mainframe they had purchased. In diplomatic language, SAP "had freed users from the pressure to implement products that make them dependent on IBM." In plain language: It would be better if customers would tie themselves to SAP rather than to IBM.

The SAP founders held on to their intention to conquer the market for standard application software. Their first contract with ICI already aimed at this target, because it explicitly allowed SAP to market the application system that had been developed for the fiber works to third-party customers. Its competitors, on the other hand, spent years undecided between developing standard software and customized proprietary software, or overspent on special fields such as automation of office work or computer integrated manufacturing. SAP chose to forgo expanding its service business or taking on lucrative development of special-purpose software. Rather, from the very beginning, SAP used each new order as a way of updating its software to represent the most relevant business processes step by step and to develop in this way a highly integrated standard software product. "The best semifinished product," mocked experts on software industry. "Well, of course we learned with each implementation," commented Tschira.

The introduction of SAP's first-generation software at Freuden-berg, Jacobs Kaffee, and Grundig at first raised "considerable technical problems," Hasso Plattner acknowledges. Simultaneously, it already showed how such bottlenecks could be avoided in the future by using new, more powerful mainframes and a specific software system that was developed by IBM for controlling databases and dialogs. Therefore, in 1978 SAP started to rewrite its R/1 system for the next generation of hardware.

SAP put the first computer of its own—a Siemens mainframe 7738 (operating system: BS 2000)—into operation in 1980 after moving into the first building of its own, a two-story affair on Max Planck Street, in the industrial area of Walldorf. In the same year the company extended its hardware by purchasing an IBM 370 and an IBM 4341. The Siemens computer as well as the IBM 370 had 2 MB of main memory; the IBM 4341 had 4 MB. In comparison, in 1997 almost no PC was offered with less than 16 MB RAM.

"In round-the-clock work on our first computer, we revised the total concept of the software," says Hasso Plattner. Fifty terminals were connected with the system on which the software package R/2 was developed. The larger main memory of the new-generation hardware made it possible, for example, to buffer more dialog information, thereby simplifying and speeding up the program. R/2 was based on a so-called basic system, so that it could be used not only on IBM computers but also on Siemens computers. This basic system served as an adapter for different operating systems. "Just about everything in this software had to be reprogrammed," says Plattner.

The Withdrawal of Wellenreuther

By 1980 it had become evident why Claus Wellenreuther performed his strange ritual of hanging from the door frame after meetings: to relieve his painful, inflamed spinal joints. Wellenreuther suffered from an insidious disease that rigidifies the spine and makes the least physical movement exceedingly painful, but it took six to seven years—even with state-of-the-art diagnostic methods—before he received a clear diagnosis: Bechterew's disease, also called ankylosing spondylitis. This condition, named after the Russian neurologist Wladimir von Bechterew (1857–1927), is an incurable disease that is assumed to be the result of an infection, presumably viral, that sets off an immunologic reaction that inflames and then stiffens the joints of the spine. The disease takes a great toll on its sufferers, and by 1980 Wellenreuther could no longer summon up the energy to deal with the firm's demands. "Wellenreuther was seriously ill," remembers Dietmar Hopp. "He had constant pain. At that time, to be involved meant to be at the scene of the action. He could not do that because he needed medical treatment."

Wellenreuther did not have the stamina for anything new at that time, and in fact he believed he would not live more than another year or two. So he left the company on March 1, 1980, under the disability clause of his contract, receiving a payment of $550,000. The users of the financial accounting system he developed were given a special offer to switch to the RF system.

Not long after leaving SAP, however, Wellenreuther heard of a new therapy, and his physical deterioration ceased. The man with the unchanged preference for Porsches considers that he has been granted "a second life" through this therapy.

Wellenreuther's new firm, DCW, now specializes in financial accounting software for midrange IBM computers of the AS/400 series. Its customers are well-known companies such as Alfa Laval, Nike, Escada, and Joop. Claus Wellenreuther was one of the guests at SAP's twenty-fifth-anniversary ceremony in April 1997 in Mannheim. On this occasion Dietmar Hopp once more paid tribute to the merits of Wellenreuther, software pioneer and SAP cofounder.

One of the five cofounders was absent from the celebration, however, and his name was not mentioned at all. Hans-Werner Hector had left the firm just four months earlier, in December 1996, amidst controversy. But there is more to tell before we reach that point in the story.

The Mainframe Version: SAP R/2

The development of the mainframe software R/2 was finished in 1981. "The system is totally new," SAP proudly told the trade press. But 1981 was also the year in which IBM introduced the first PC, and what software experts did not realize was at that moment in the United States, the next phase of the computer revolution had already been initiated. The impact of this innovation was that a decade later mainframe technology would be replaced by a network of midrange computers, workstations, and PCs. This trend plunged IBM—by then market-dominating—into a crisis. The irony was that this development had been caused by Big Blue itself.

At IBM, the engineer John Cooke already in 1974 had designed the first RISC (reduced instruction set computing) machine. The central processor of this type of computer, in contrast to conventional mainframes that were based on CISC (complete instruction set computing) architecture, worked with a stock of built-in standard instructions that was reduced by 50 percent from the CISC set. (Today's state-of-the-art PC processors, such as the Intel's Pentium series, are based on a mixed system, the so-called Harvard architecture.)

Like a racing bicycle, which is faster because it is built without fenders, headlight, bell, or basket to add extra weight, through the RISC architecture the speed of a processor could be improved considerably. In 1982 Andreas Bechtolsheim and his fellow student Scott McNealy established the computer firm Sun Microsystems in Silicon Valley. Their intention was to manufacture computers based on RISC architecture that could be used under the "open" operating system Unix, which was not dependent on IBM, Siemens, or another hardware manufacturer. In 1987 Sun introduced its high-performance Sparc workstation and abruptly changed the market for commercial hardware. Soon networks of servers and workstations had taken on some of the burden of data processing. In later years, as PCs got more powerful, often just a single standard PC was sufficient for this purpose.

Like many other companies, including IBM itself, SAP was surprised by the PC trend. As Hasso Plattner told the newsmagazine *Der Spiegel*, "In the 1980s we were too close to IBM and therefore were too strongly fixated on mainframes. At first we couldn't believe that a new megatrend had arisen."

After the introduction of R/2, its new mainframe software, SAP increasingly left implementation and program maintenance to specially selected consulting firms that had specific knowledge about a given sector of industry. Very early, for example, EDV-Studio Ploenzke, from Wiesbaden (now CSC Ploenzke AG, a subsidiary of Computer Sciences Corporation in El Segundo, California), took on the implementation of SAP software. In 1982 another alliance was agreed upon, this time with Organisation Plaut AG, in order to strengthen the financial accounting aspect of the software.

This was and still is a lucrative business for consultants. Capital expenditures for new hardware and standard software were planned over periods of ten to fifteen years. "At first the financial accounting system was implemented," explained Paul-Michael Dahlheim, the spokesperson for Price Waterhouse in Europe and manager in charge of the partnership with SAP. "In the next year the cost accounting system was implemented, then fixed-asset accounting, order processing, and materials and logistics management. And at some time or other production planning was implemented. Thus, the implementation of standard software was a process that dragged on for six to eight years."

By pursuing this strategy of partnerships with consulting firms, however, SAP left itself open to certain problems that strongly influenced the image of the firm. In 1986 a confidential internal memo warned: "The good reputation of our products and above all the efficiency of their use suffer from high implementation and especially maintenance costs." More than a decade later, experts on the software industry still think that the future of SAP will primarily depend on the answer to the following question: Which organizational and technical solutions will the company come up with to reduce these costs—without annoying its consulting-firm partners?

With R/2, SAP took the lead at large enterprises. "Almost unnoticed by the general public, with the modular standard software package R/2 SAP succeeded in establishing a quasi-monopolistic position on the market for commercial enterprise software for IBM 370 mainframes in Germany," commented *Computerwoche* in 1990. In 1996 the R/2 system, which will be enhanced, maintained, and supported through the year 2004, included the following modules:

- RA   Fixed-asset accounting
- RF   Financial accounting
- RK   Cost accounting
- RK-P   Project management
- RM   Maintenance and repair
- RM-Mat   Materials and logistics management
- RM-PPS   Production planning
- RM-QSS   Quality management
- RP   Human resources management
- RV   Sales, invoicing, shipment

As of December 1997, about 1,400 companies were still using the R/2 system on mainframe computers as their business software solution. Releases 6.0 and 6.1 are the latest examples of the improved range of R/2 system functionality.

Experts on the software industry assessed the caution with which the firm expanded in the development phase as a crucial factor in its success. "I think it was very good for us that we could concentrate during this period on developing our products—without the problems and troubles that are involved in a rapid expansion," muses Dietmar Hopp.

From 1982 to 1984 SAP hired dozens of new employees who had just received their doctorates. One of the first hired in 1982 was a physicist, Henning Kagermann.

"We're in the wave of those who came ten years after the company was founded," says Kagermann, who was promoted to a spot on the board of directors in 1991 and was put in charge of software development for financial accounting and for industry solutions. In 1993 and 1996 other members of the second SAP generation, including Peter Zencke, Gerhard Oswald, Claus Heinrich, and Paul Wahl, also took seats on the board. Their contribution had been to help design the latest software package, R/3, which brought SAP a breakthrough on the world market in 1992.

As with the development of its software, in establishing a presence in foreign markets SAP was led step by step by the needs of its customers and partners. This took place in two phases:

- In 1978 John Deere, the United States manufacturer of agricultural machinery with a branch in Mannheim, decided to implement the SAP financial accounting system in its European and African subsidiaries. The tractor manufacturer even translated the software into French on its own. "This customer exported us," says Hasso Plattner. For SAP, this was the start of its move into international accounting. Different ways of handling payments, difficult currencies, and country-specific accounting standards all had to be taken into account.
- In 1984, in Biel, Switzerland, SAP (International) AG was founded. This company was intended to coordinate foreign business relating to R/2. Because R/2 could be used on mainframe computers from Siemens under the operating system BS 2000, Siemens chose to implement SAP R/2 worldwide. This was the second phase of internationalization.

The overseas business was largely developed by the Swiss manager Hans Schlegel, who—coming from Hilti AG, in the principality of Liechtenstein—started with SAP in 1984. Before he left SAP in 1993, as a member of the board, Schlegel was in charge of international sales. When he took his position at SAP, Schlegel clearly indicated the scope of his vision when he announced, "My intention is that one day taxi drivers in Philadelphia or Singapore will know where to go, just as the drivers in Heidelberg do, when I say: 'To SAP, please.'"

Traffic Jam

Some United States investment clubs recommend that their members occasionally drive past the headquarters of companies whose stock interests them. From the number of cars in the parking lot—especially after normal working hours—or from the presence of construction work, conclusions can be drawn about the future stock price of that company. In Germany there are at least five thousand clubs of small investors, and for their members, the industrial area in Walldorf is worth a visit.

"There's a traffic jam every morning and evening" because of the number of people going to work at SAP's offices, complains Gerhard Mayer, a fifty-six-year-old local resident. It seems that on every second corner is an SAP office building or one of its parking garages. During the week some 4,300 employees drive into the industrial area every day. On any given day there are over a thousand people undergoing training at SAP, as well as several hundred customers and employees of SAP's partner firms. Additionally, the employees of the other firms in the industrial area—for example, Heidelberger Druck—must be considered. The result is "really a traffic disaster," adds Mayer.

"On the other hand, everybody benefits from SAP," says retailer Rolf Kübler, age forty-seven. In 1988 SAP opened its international training center, and since then, thousands of software developers, IT consultants, and employees of partner firms and customers from all over the world have come to Walldorf to familiarize themselves with SAP software.

Hotels and restaurants throughout the region have benefited from this "software tourism"; new hotels have even been constructed. Nevertheless, many hotels regularly have 90 percent of their rooms booked with SAP guests. "In spite of a well-developed infrastructure with hotels, from Monday to Friday it is difficult to get a room because all the hotels are booked up," the mayor of Walldorf warned at one point. The retail trade and service industries as well as the construction industry are all benefiting from the high-tech boom in the region, reported the *Rhine-Neckar-Zeitung*.

In order to temper the annoyance of local residents, who were suffering from SAP-related traffic jams, the software giant contributed some $570,000 to the construction of a third lane on one of the area's main roads. Additionally, the company began giving its employees passes for public transport, and it established a company-owned shuttle service using minibuses. This should improve the situation, and the municipality of Walldorf also has plans to undertake some road improvements at its own expense. "Unusual developments require unusual actions," explains Wilhelm Schneider, town clerk and town architect.

"The success of SAP is a wonder, and its headquarters on the outskirts of Walldorf is a wonder in itself," wrote the magazine *Stern* in 1995. And while SAP has undertaken many building projects in the area—its facilities manager, Ewald Engelbert, is regarded as a sort of low-profile sovereign in the area and has made quite a few farmers very happy by buying their land at a great premium—more needs to be done. After constructing its training center, the company built a six-story development and sales center, which opened in 1992, and a parking garage with 1,600 parking spaces. The headquarters of SAP has been added to seven times since 1980 but is still bursting at the seams, even after the construction of a new office building for six hundred employees recently.

Because many of SAP's buildings are rather far apart, daily internal SAP communication is primarily based on e-mail, and the company will need to rely on it even more heavily in the future. Via MLP—that is the name of this office communication system, which is based on SAP software—CEO Hopp and the other board members are accessible to their employees. "We cannot do without e-mail," explains Anton Dillinger, who has worked at SAP since 1978 and is therefore one of the veterans. "Direct communication might have worked in the initial phase, but it's no longer practical when a company grows."

SAP City

Whether SAP will be able to keep up with the global Internet business is no abstract question for the inhabitants of Walldorf. When something happens with SAP—its stock price goes down or up or some internal upheaval occurs—there is only one topic of discussion in Walldorf.

But the chances that SAP—and Walldorf—will continue to prosper in "SAP City" seem good. In front of the Hotel Vorfelder waves the flag of Europe, and all of the continent will need to convert to the euro. Companies worldwide will manage the shift to the new currency by means of specially developed SAP software. But internationality at SAP is not limited to foreign currency accounting and conversions—it has a more personal meaning. In 1993 the newspaper *Mannheimer Morgen* awarded a prize to an advertisement, developed by employees of SAP and financed through private donations (including one from Dietmar Hopp), that spoke out against hostility toward foreigners in Germany.

"Our message is clear," says the mayor of Walldorf. "We are interlocked internationally. Our wealth is based on this." Beginning with John Jacob Astor, who was in a sense an early international businessman himself, and continuing through to the present day with SAP, the town of Walldorf does indeed have a role to play in the internationalization of the future.

And the boom has just started in Walldorf. The reason for the optimistic forecast of *Manager Magazin* is the unparalleled success of the SAP R/3 system.

Part II

PRODUCTS, SERVICES, AND MARKETS—CORE COMPETENCIES

Chapter Three

SAP R/3—Product Development and Customers

Our most important and absolutely right decision was in 1987–88, when we decided to develop R/3. By then, mainframe computers were at their peak and the demand for R/2 was booming. In fact, we could have rested on our laurels. But we were tempted to develop a multiplatform software— and luckily for us, because use of mainframe computers dramatically declined shortly after.

—Dietmar Hopp

Case Study: Vobis Microcomputer

For years, salesclerks in the computer stores of Vobis Microcomputer AG in Germany were known disparagingly by PC buyers and trade publications as "box pushers." They had little time and less patience for customers looking for advice. The computers and accessories they sold were hustled from the truck ramp into the storeroom and then over the counter, and customers had little opportunity to check the merchandise. Nor did the customers always receive what they had selected from the catalog, but usually they didn't find this out until they got home and opened the box. (Ironically enough, the company's name, Vobis, is from Latin and means "for you.")

But things have changed at Vobis. Now the customer is treated as if he were there to buy a BMW instead of a printer cable or a monitor. The customer's order is configured on a computer terminal in the store and transmitted via ISDN digital network or satellite to

Vobis headquarters in Würselen, Germany. The customer can then pick up his new PC, configured exactly as he wanted it, usually within forty-eight hours.

This sophisticated computer-based production planning and sales system ensures that what is delivered corresponds to the invoice—for example, a minitower PC with 64 MB RAM, 17-inch color monitor, and software package 1. It has also substantially reduced the inventory Vobis needs to keep, and has shortened delivery time as well. The system has allowed Europe's largest chain of computer stores to strongly increase its lead, emphasized Heribert Kraus, head of the organization and data processing section at Vobis. In 1996 the company (a subsidiary of Kaufhof, the department store division of the Metro group) became the leader in the German PC market.

Most customers do not know that their Vobis PC was custom-manufactured using the just-in-time production technique, which in turn is made possible by SAP software. This example illustrates how the decentralized use of state-of-the-art enterprise software simultaneously changes management, manufacturing, logistics, and service. The Vobis installation is one of 13,400 worldwide R/3 installations (as of December 1997). The latest and most powerful software package from Walldorf was praised as the business software version of the Swiss Army knife by the magazine *Datamation.*

The powerful software system by which business processes can be planned, controlled, and analyzed is contained on two CD-ROMS. SAP R/3 was installed for the first time in Germany in July 1992. This is not software that will be obsolete tomorrow. Rather, customers can benefit from technology and business practices that represent the state of the art.

The main difference between R/3 and its predecessor, R/2, is that the new generation of software does not use mainframe computers. Costing $920 million to develop, R/3 was targeted to smaller computers (servers), workstations, and standard PCs that share the burden of data processing according to client-server architecture. In this way, processes that previously took hours or even days can be handled in seconds on the screen of a PC. The highly complex software presents itself as a Windows program that can be used with a click of a mouse. "With R/3 we had the right product at the right time," explains CEO Hasso Plattner.

While the mainframe version, R/2, will be enhanced, maintained, and supported by SAP through 2004, R/3 release 3.0 by far exceeds the functionality of its predecessor. Originally SAP had planned R/3 as a variant of R/2 for midsized enterprises. But right from the start large enterprises whose mainframe-based data processing was too bulky for global competition pounced on R/3. Customers can choose from a dozen main R/3 modules—for example, financial accounting (FI), controlling (CO), and human resources (HR).

This range of standard software is supplemented by many special-purpose programs—for example, for connecting sales representatives using cellular phones. Also, in close cooperation with consulting partners and market leaders in different sectors of industry, SAP developed industry-specific solutions that are extensions of the core R/3 system for industries such as chemical, high-tech, consumer goods, automotive, insurance, retail, pharmaceutical, banking, and telecommunications.

Country-specific user menus ensure that the software can be used all over the world—in United States, Japanese, or European corporate headquarters as well as in a Mexican plant or at a supplier in China. Not only can standard R/3 modules be linked in a company or industrial group, but also standard interfaces enable on-line data transmission between different R/3 users around the globe. The standard software from Germany serves as a sort of IT pacemaker in the globalization process.

Through R/3 the overseas business of SAP got its crucial push—beginning in the United States in 1993, where it has the reputation of being a top-quality product of German engineering skills, much like German autos. Oddly enough, while in 1994 Hasso Plattner was named one of the top fifty R & D stars by the United States magazine *Industry Week* for SAP's revolutionary software, in Germany the R/3 concept was receiving harsh criticism. Soon even *Computerwoche* commented that the "complexity of R/3 is fatal for SAP." Annoyed,

SAP overreacted, trying to refute the criticism with letter-to-the-editor campaigns and, eventually, an advertising boycott.

But apparently the software's users didn't find its complexity overwhelming. In 1995 200,000 people worldwide used SAP software. In 1997, it was already more than 1.5 million. And this is despite the software's high cost: The R/3 software license is acquired for functional blocks, and its cost depends on the number of users. In 1996 the license fee per job was between $2,700 and $4,000. For a complete installation of hardware and software, a midsized enterprise must pay several hundred thousand dollars. Large enterprises that install R/3 company-wide often pay a fee in the tens of millions of dollars. For Vobis, for example, the cost for converting its computer manufacturing and sales to the R/3 modules—logistics/sales and distribution (SD), materials management (MM), and production planning (PP)—was $14 million.

The idea that Vobis could improve its performance this way came from Theo Lieven, the founder and former CEO of Vobis, who presented it at a management conference in May 1995. At the time, Vobis used continuous series–type production. PCs were built to sales forecasts, and the final configuration of the PCs was made in the Vobis retail outlets. When they discussed how they could reduce stock in the retail outlets and simultaneously serve customers better and more quickly, Lieven used the magic word *on-line*, arguing that the optimal solution would be a data processing system that could transmit order data from the retail outlets directly to headquarters in Würselen.

The Vobis founder maintained that by reducing the expenses of carrying inventories and shortening delivery time for PCs in this way, Vobis would have a real competitive advantage. The company has more than 1,100 retail outlets in eleven European countries—of which 340 are in Germany. Faced with competition from other chain stores, department stores, specialty computer stores, and mail-order companies, Vobis wanted to "offer the customers a service that our competitors absolutely could not offer," narrates Ulrich Flatten, the controller of Vobis.

Together with his colleague Heribert Kraus, Flatten proposed to implement the R/3 logistics module. Vobis already used the R/3 modules for financial accounting (FI), controlling (CO), and fixed-asset accounting (AM). The SAP logistics module for configuration management had been developed for manufacturers with a large product range, and it appealed to the Vobis team. Their plan was to support the total ordering, manufacturing, and sales chain through R/3, from specifying the appropriate PC configuration (with automatic blocks that would prevent the combination of incompatible components) to pricing, ordering, manufacturing, and shipment. The resulting business data could be analyzed with other R/3 modules—for example, financial accounting.

This meant, however, that Vobis had to totally revamp its logistics. "All our operations had to be analyzed and harmonized with the new requirements," explains project manager Kraus. To this end, consultants were brought in to estimate how much it would cost and how long it would take.

For Vobis the estimate was facilitated by the fact that the company already used R/3 in different subdomains. Based on a detailed analysis of the actual situation, the experts estimated that the built-to-order concept could be implemented within three months. In order to carry this out, the Vobis board got involved—even Lieven took a part in reorganizing manufacturing and sales. Seventeen project teams were established that tackled the varied tasks of the R/3 project. One was to control parts inventory through switching to the just-in-time principle. But first, the central warehouse of Vobis had to be reorganized.

For example, new transport equipment had to be purchased, and the production line equipment had to be replaced. Moreover, a bar-code system was installed that allowed complete job control via scanners. The SAP logistics software contains an early-warning system that can indicate possible undesirable developments and bottle-necks in the production sequence before they cause a crisis. In order to prevent such situations from occurring, the R/3 production planning module can be used. This can determine the requirements for materials, machines, and employees. When there is an increased inflow of orders—for example, as a consequence of a successful regional advertising campaign—the software helps to determine within seconds which production teams still have free production capacity to cushion such order peaks.

The company planned to produce five thousand PCs per day in the initial phase. Some one thousand R/3 users—from salesclerks in the retail outlets to product managers—had to be linked to the computer network. Only in this way could they take advantage of the highly integrated system. The benefit was that everyone had access to current planning, production, and sales data. For example, marketing specialists in headquarters could analyze the sales impact of a new TV commercial just by looking at their PC screen. Simultaneously, the salesclerk feeding in the order data could find out whether a particular multimedia PC would be delivered in four days or only two days.

Vobis' computer network needed to master an enormous volume of data. Meanwhile, customers could choose between dozens of PC types, with a huge number of hardware and software options for each. For single-item production supported by R/3 module SD, a bill of materials processor (BOMP) that also has control functions was developed. This allows the system to recognize when the stock of components for a particular product line drops below a previously defined critical limit, thereby automatically triggering a purchase order for the needed materials. The implemented R/3 system is based on this principle of event-controlled process chains.

But Vobis was surprised by the computer-memory requirements this would entail. Previously, Vobis had managed with a single mid-sized computer from Hewlett-Packard as a server running R/3. But now the SAP consultants estimated that the future data volume would be more than this computer could handle. The new data volume would need to be distributed to twelve Unix-based high-performance servers from Hewlett-Packard. These, in turn, could serve in real time a thousand standard PCs as clients. Soon Heribert Kraus understood the challenge of his task: "By then, this was the largest R/3 implementation in a client-server environment in Germany," remembers the Vobis project manager. The Vobis team realized with a shock that it lacked both the resources and the know-how to manage this transition on its own.

Fortunately, in this stage of the project Vobis found out that it was an advantage to be a member of the club of sophisticated R/3 users: Special detachments of staff from SAP and Hewlett-Packard (which was a longtime partner of SAP and supplier of Vobis) saw to it that the innovation push did not get stuck at the beginning. Hewlett-Packard, as a leading manufacturer of Unix-based computers for client-server networks, had already contributed to the development of R/3 software. Meanwhile, Hewlett-Packard, as an SAP logo partner, benefited from the worldwide hardware, software, and consulting business linked with SAP enterprise software. "Without HP, the development could not have taken its rapid course," emphasizes Hasso Plattner, the author of R/3.

Hewlett-Packard, a pioneer in open systems, was one of the factors behind SAP's decision to switch its software from IBM to Unix-based computers. Through this dramatic shift in policy SAP rose to the status of a global enterprise.

Unix-Based Open System Architecture

Originally the intention of the SAP founders was that R/3 should be used on a new class of midrange IBM computers—the AS/400 series. Big Blue particularly wanted to position this computer, which was controlled by a proprietary operating system, in midsized companies. But at the last moment, reports Plattner, SAP pulled the helm around and decided on Unix because the IBM system showed a poor performance with the complex R/3 system.

Up until the early 1990s, SAP had been regarded as a loyal vassal of IBM, and sold its R/2 software mostly to large enterprises. The idea for a new generation of software that would be custom-made for use in subsidiaries of industrial groups and midsized enterprises at first basically followed the IBM model, too. Dietmar Hopp, Hasso Plattner, and Klaus Tschira developed this concept on their way home from an IBM conference in Frankfurt, where IBM had presented its new system application architecture (SAA). The SAA was designed to standardize for the first time all IBM computers and their operating systems—from PCs to midrange computers to mainframes. In the future, developing software would be simplified substantially—at least for the IBM world—because all application software would be written in the programming language C.

C had been developed in the early 1970s in AT&T's Bell Laboratories. Both the Unix operating system (the archetype of which had been invented by AT&T) and most application software that ran under Unix were written in C. This programming language was enjoying increased popularity.

The SAA computer architecture used relational databases. At that time most mainframe computing (including R/2) relied on hierarchical database systems, which had a simpler structure but could store information only according to a rigid pattern. This was particularly suited to standardized, recurring information requests. The SAP experts believed that it should be possible in the next generation of their enterprise software to link and to analyze company data more flexibly. It should enable users to poll data more easily in combinations that could not be foreseen at the time the software was installed.

After the IBM conference in Frankfurt, for the SAP founders it was a foregone conclusion that SAA would determine the future of SAP software. The new software architecture would demand a huge commitment of financial, personnel, and technical resources from SAP because every aspect of the software would need to be rewritten. Though it would be a big task, the SAP cofounders were confident: "It was a cloudy day, but we were totally high on our way back," remembers Plattner.

Unix is the open (that is, independent of any specific computer manufacturer) operating system for high-performance network computers that are based on 32-bit processors. Unix was already the preferred operating system at universities and in research institutes, but at that time, it played only a minor role as far as SAP's plans were concerned. Data processing in companies and public administration was still dominated by mainframe and midrange computers from manufacturers such as IBM, Siemens, or Digital Equipment Corporation (DEC) that could be used only with their proprietary operating systems. IT professionals often regarded Unix as something left to the academics and did not regard it as an operating system to be taken seriously for corporate computing.

SAP, which was closely connected with IBM and Siemens, took the same view—at least publicly. The SAP founders were anxious not to shake the confidence of their IBM-dependent R/2 users in the future safety of SAP software. Therefore, in November 1987 Dietmar Hopp promptly responded with an angry letter to the editor when the magazine *Computerwoche* came up with the headline "Unix Ahead of SAA: SAP Changes Its Software Strategy." The journal reported on supposed differences between IBM and SAP about SAA and the role of Unix. The background was that Hasso Plattner had let slip that SAP was developing the new system to run under Unix. But after the *Computerwoche* article appeared, SAP quickly disassociated itself from the notion, and Hopp expressly emphasized: "We did not change our software strategy and do not prefer Unix to SAA." However, seven years later Hopp came up with a slightly different version of the beginning of R/3. In 1994, in a lecture at the university in Karlsruhe, Hopp said: "SAP had decided already in 1987 to develop a new generation of SAP software based on the Unix operating system. That was a crucial decision, because it implied a high financial risk; in 1987 nobody could know how the Unix market would develop."

In any case, SAP wrote the initial version of R/3 in both C and SAP's own programming language, ABAP/4. It intended to present the new software for the first time at the computer show CeBIT in Hannover, on an IBM mainframe. A database system for IBM computers had been adjusted for this purpose. But in the test runs it turned out that neither the IBM mainframe nor the IBM database system could handle the sophisticated SAP software. "The performance was so bad," recalls Hasso Plattner, "that the entire team refused to finish up the work and said they would not demonstrate the product at the Hannover show. I replied that we had to pick up the pieces and start over again."

The SAP software professionals had just six weeks until the CeBIT show, but they rose to Plattner's challenge. Plattner recalls that Peter Zencke was the first one to break the silence in the room.

Zencke, a member of the R/3 core team, had been with SAP since 1984 and was in charge of R/3 development. "Why shouldn't we do it the other way around? Instead of trying to run all the programs on the largest available computer, let's see if we can do it on a smaller one," suggested Zencke. He meant a Digital Equipment Corporation workstation, the DEC 5000. This was hardly larger than a desktop PC, ran Unix, and was already being used at SAP for developing R/3 modules.

In order to use the fast minicomputer as a server for R/3, the complete IBM database had to be transferred to the Unix-compatible database system produced by the United States software provider Oracle. Plattner decided to go with Zencke's suggestion, and, as he recalls, "Fifteen employees shouted for joy because they were Unix fans and disliked the mainframe anyhow. They got right to work— the pressure was really intense," remembered Plattner. But the SAP team managed to deliver a demonstration version of R/3 for Unix in time for the computer show.

Years after the SAP presentation of R/3 at the CeBIT show, Plattner is still radiant as he recalls the response of the show visitors to the change of software policy. Gerhard Oswald, with SAP since 1981, demonstrated to the CeBIT audience how much highly complex software could be packed into an inconspicuous Unix computer. "This tiny machine with a few extra disk memories—it was really ridiculous," says Hasso Plattner with a laugh.

But the message at CeBIT in 1991 was this: "You can do without a mainframe computer." The visitors were more fascinated by the fact that the new generation of software could be scaled to operate on workstations than by the new software itself.

As a flawless client-server solution based on Unix, R/3 exploits the main advantage of state-of-the-art server systems: The high-performance processors and state-of-the-art network operating systems are designed so that several workstations can be linked to a single system. The computing power of such a system can outdo even huge mainframe computers. That means that R/3 installations can be scaled flexibly to the requirements and size of each user. In the past, a company that wanted to be prepared for the future had either to install an expensive, oversized computer system at the start or go with a smaller system intially and then undergo a costly upgrade later.

But the R/3 system could accommodate the addition of several hundred or even thousand additional PC clients to the existing server network. Hasso Plattner explains the sensational success of R/3 by the fact "that we selected a technology that allows us to scale up and down to an extent not known ever before. Nowadays, R/3 scales higher than R/2."

But after the successful demonstration at CeBIT, SAP was put under strong pressure to produce a shipping version of R/3 in a very short time frame. It would be necessary to marry the voluminous R/3 software, with its millions of lines of code, to Unix in a flawless way in order to keep the promises made at CeBIT. Although the DEC workstation they had used for the demonstration carried out 20 million instructions per second, it was already working to capacity. The complete R/3 system would require much more computing power.

"And again, we had luck as far as computer performance was concerned," remembers Hopp. "The processors that had just come out for Unix computers broke all thinkable limits." He was referring to Hewlett-Packard's newest Unix workstation, the HP 720, which also had been shown at CeBIT. Capable of processing 50 million instructions per second, the performance of this workstation was more than double the performance of the DEC computer. HP helped SAP out of a fix by promising express delivery of several truckloads of the new equipment to be used in program development in Walldorf. "Two hundred workstations were delivered within six weeks," recalls Plattner.

A year and a half later, in July 1992, the finished R/3 system was ready to ship in Germany. The new software could be used on Unix-based workstations from Bull, DEC, Hewlett-Packard, IBM, and Siemens Nixdorf. (However, it could not yet be used on the IBM AS/400, with its proprietary operating system OS/400.) Moreover, R/3 could be adjusted to new server types and network operating systems in a short time. This was proved by SAP in the following years. For example, in 1993 R/3 was adjusted to run under Windows NT, Microsoft's successful rival to Unix.

The adaptability of R/3 was achieved by its modular structure for three-tier client-server computing. This can perhaps be seen best in the details of the R/3 installation at Vobis.

- **Level 1: Database Server** R/3 can be used with databases from Oracle, Microsoft, IBM, Informix, or Software AG. On this server there are several thousand tables (SAP-speak: "transparent tables") that control the R/3 data management. Vobis selected an HP 9000/T500 as a database server.

- **Level 2: R/3 Application Server** In larger installations, several networked workstations are used—for example, Vobis uses eleven Unix-based HP servers. The application server contains the core of the R/3 system. These are programmed basic business processes. R/3 application modules for different business processes are based on this core. The system core controls the cooperation of the different R/3 modules.

- **Level 3: Presentation Servers** Mostly these are standard PCs running Windows, where R/3 can be used by mouse click. These PCs show the user a pleasant graphical user interface and can present company data in color and in diagrams.

In 1992 SAP became the first provider of enterprise software to use a state-of-the-art graphical user interface. Its competitors (and its own R/2) still had to struggle with text-oriented screen masks from the mainframe era. Particularly in the PC-minded United States, this competitive advantage contributed considerably to the success of R/3. For example, Bruce Richardson, of the consulting and market research firm Advanced Manufacturing Research, in Boston, Massachusetts, noted that SAP "was able to come in and show a 20-minute 'drive-by' with a beautiful front end; and it just blew away the green-screen competition."

The heavy-duty framework of R/3 is hidden behind the tidied-up facade. But because no enterprise exactly resembles any other and most companies need only parts of the built-in R/3 business processes, the software must be adjusted at each implementation—in technical jargon, "parameterized." Vobis, for example, already in 1996 had a data volume of 300 GB. In order to ensure smooth R/3 data traffic, a complex "schedule" was required so that data could be retrieved as needed.

What SAP calls "transparent tables" serve as a schedule for R/3. These tables contain thousands of switching variables that must be customized before the R/3 system can be put into operation. For payroll accounting alone, for example, a hundred tables must be filled out. These variables determine which data can be produced or retrieved for which business processes, and by which user or program function. So the user company must define the order processing process, the cost centers, or how additional R/3 modules should work together with already installed modules. Vobis, for example, had to define how the new modules for logistics and production planning interacted with the existing controlling software.

In adjusting the highly integrated R/3 software to the needs of their individual enterprise, a company's IT professionals mostly depend on external R/3 specialists who know all about R/3's complexities. One single control field that is wrongly filled out can have a direct impact on the program run, and so competent R/3 consultants are among the experts in greatest demand on the IT labor market. But all this means that implementation costs for R/3 can be very high.

"The complexity of R/3 is fatal for SAP," said the trade journal *Computerwoche* just before the CeBIT computer show in 1995. In a provocative article that caused a hot discussion, R/3 expert Karl Schmitz, from Hamburg, gave the reasons why, in his opinion, "the future of SAP has already come to an end." He pleaded for a more flexible software structure—that is, object-oriented programming. In this approach certain basic functions are "encapsulated" in easy-to-grasp program modules that can be combined in different ways, like building blocks. Schmitz took the view that SAP's R/3 and comparable software systems had no future: "These programs will literally choke to death on their own complexity."

SAP overreacted to this criticism. One reason was that the business magazine *Wirtschaftswoche* took advantage of these polemics to run a spectacular leading article in which they imputed unfair business practices to SAP. As SAP saw it, all this had started with the article in *Computerwoche*. SAP spokesman Michael Pfister outlined the company's response this way: "Because SAP's future according to *Computerwoche* has already come to an end, SAP therefore has no business being in a high-tech journal, and so will reduce its advertisements considerably. We try to avoid exposing ourselves to the reproach that we influence editorial content through our advertisements, which had a volume of $494,000 in 1994."

However touchy SAP's external reaction, internally it was felt that the criticism of R/3 as overly complex was justified. So all levels at SAP began a drive to considerably simplify the implementation of SAP R/3 and reduce implementation costs. (This will be explored at greater length later in the book.)

There is no doubt that R/3 is complex, and SAP consultants tend to indulge in a little gallows humor when it comes to adjusting the R/3 system. CSC Ploenzke AG, one of the largest consulting partners of SAP, circulated a jokey flow chart describing typical problems of R/3 implementation. It started with the question "Does SAP R/3 work?" The answer "No" leads to the question "Will you be blamed?" If you answer "Yes" to that question, you are taken to a box that reads "Poor you." If the first question, however, is answered "Yes," the arrow leads to a box with this recommendation: "Don't fiddle around with it—then everything will be all right."

The complexity issue aside, SAP's clients tend to be happy with their installations. At Vobis, only three months after the start of the project, the first production planning and sales system was "productive" (SAP-speak). Vobis expressly praised "the good support from SAP" without which the project could not have been carried out.

A customer who selects a new PC in the Vobis store unknowingly triggers a huge R/3 chain reaction. The PC configuration for the customer is determined with an R/3 special-purpose configurator program, and it will be checked on-line to see whether and how quickly the required components can be delivered. The customer receives a printed confirmation that covers all details of the order. Then the order will be transmitted via satellite or ISDN to the Vobis data processing center in Würselen, which processes the data for production.

Barely twenty minutes later, production can start in the factory. The components selected by the customer are pulled from the high-tech warehouse and passed on to the assembly line. R/3 completely documents the passage of the new PC from assembly to the loading of software selected by the buyer to quality control to the shipping department. Software for quality management—specifically developed on behalf of Vobis with an interface to production planning software—ensures that the PC exactly meets Vobis' requirements and high quality standards.

The PCs and peripherals are packed according to a sophisticated, sequentially controlled method on pallets of different size in order to use truck freight capacity optimally. "We reduced the delivery time to two days and shrank our inventory by 20 percent," says Vobis' project manager.

With his new Vobis computer—which perhaps includes a Pentium II chip from Intel (an R/3 user itself), a monitor from Philips (an SAP customer), Windows 98 from Microsoft (an R/3 user and SAP partner), a printer from HP (an R/3 user and SAP partner also), a speech recognition system from IBM (another R/3 user and SAP partner), and a modem from Motorola (yet another R/3 user), the PC user can surf the Internet. Perhaps he will stumble across the Web site of the

Taronga Park Zoo in Sydney, Australia. What he may not know is that since the spring of 1996, the kangaroos at the zoo are managed by R/3 software from Walldorf, too. SAP cofounder Hasso Plattner made this technological leap possible by delivering the software free of charge. The computer—a midrange high-performance IBM AS/400 with a 64-bit processor—was donated by IBM. The Taronga Park Zoo was used as a test installation in 1996 when R/3 was adapted to the IBM computer for which the software had originally been planned. But the kangaroos don't know this, either.

Chapter Four

Positioning in the High-End Market Segment

If you compete with companies that are heavy users of information technologies, that can move to a time-effective competitive operation and you do not embrace that same technology, you will be beaten to the punch every time, in terms of time, in terms of information richness and effectiveness.

—ANDY GROVE

SAP's Market Position

By 1996, SAP was dominating the rapidly growing market segment for client-server-based integrated enterprise software. This is largely thanks to the introduction of R/3. SAP's sales revenue reached $3.5 billion in 1997—an increase of 62 percent in comparison to 1996.

The largest software provider in Europe, SAP is ranked fourth among the top ten software providers in the world. The world market volume for enterprise software was estimated at $5.4 billion in 1996. Industry experts forecasted that this market would grow on average by approximately 30 percent each year until the year 2000.

According to a recent study by the United States market research firm International Data Corporation (IDC), in Framingham, Massachusetts, SAP has established a commanding lead for integrated

Sales Revenue of SAP AG

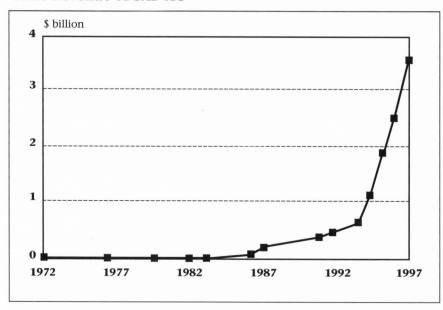

Top Ten Independent Software Providers, 1997

Rank	Company	Sales $ million	Change from previous year %	Employees	Sales per employee $ thousands
1	Microsoft Corp.	12,836	+ 39	25,000	513
2	Computer Associates	4,457	+ 13	11,209	398
3	Oracle Corp.	4,447	+ 25	33,775	132
4	SAP AG	3,468	+ 62	12,856	300
5	Novell Inc.	930	− 22	4,700	198
6	Adobe Systems Inc.	912	+ 16	2,702	340
7	Sybase Inc.	904	− 11	5,658	160
8	BMC Software Inc.	731	+ 30	2,300	318
9	SAS Institute Inc.	727	+ 15	5,108	142
10	PeopleSoft Inc.	706	+ 81	4,452	159

Source: Software Magazine

enterprise software in a client-server environment, holding a market share of 28 percent—a figure greater than the combined market shares of its next five competitors. In the European market for enterprise software, its share, 41 percent, is even stronger.

SAP is not only the world's fourth-largest software company, but also the undisputed global leader in enterprise software. The German newspaper *Handelsblatt* commented that "SAP is well on the way to establishing its software as the industry standard." *Business Week* wrote that SAP now can be considered an industry in its own right.

Sales Breakdown

In 1997 SAP's revenues were still dominated by product sales, but the growth of revenues from training and consulting (rates of 90 percent and 70 percent, respectively) were far above average. Sales of the R/3 system totaled $2.2 billion, while sales of the R/2 system declined by 8 percent, to $128.5 million.

Sales Breakdown by Type of Product and Service, 1997

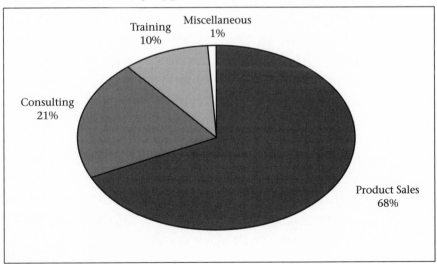

SAP Installations

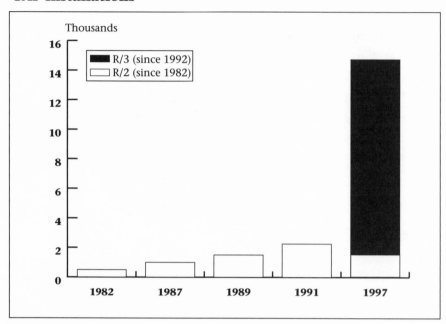

In 1997 Germany remained the company's second-largest market after the United States, where SAP sales increased by 82 percent to $1.2 billion. Sales in the Pacific Rim region grew by 69 percent.

The United States takes first place as SAP's single best sales region. In order to meet the needs of the rapidly growing market there, the staff of SAP America, Inc., grew by 67 percent, reaching 2,580 employees at the end of 1997. SAP's United States subsidiary was the first to develop AcceleratedSAP (ASAP)—a method to reduce the time and expense of R/3 system implementation by up to 50 percent. SAP supports the TeamSAP initiative that was successfully inaugurated in North America in 1997. TeamSAP offers an integrated infrastructure of people, products, and processes. SAP has taken on increased responsibility for ensuring successful R/3 implementation for its customers, and an SAP consultant or "coach" is assigned to each customer project. Dietmar Hopp forecasts that in 2005 sales will be divided about evenly between America, the Pacific Rim, and Europe.

Hopp explains this impressive success as follows: "We have been

Sales Breakdown by Region, 1997

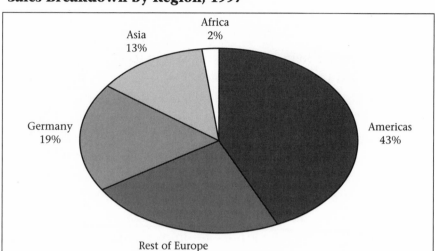

so successful because our employees are highly qualified and motivated and because we anticipated the future trends in data processing quite right." Since start-up SAP has created more than 5,516 jobs in Germany and 7,340 jobs abroad.

The impressive sales growth probably cannot be sustained because many large enterprises—the typical SAP customers—already have installed SAP software. In 1996 more than 450 of the top 500 European companies and 9 of the top 10 Fortune 500 companies were users of SAP software. The largest order in company history was placed at the end of 1995 by Deutsche Telekom, which planned to use R/3 in 30,000 jobs.

Experts on the software industry assume that midsized firms soon will be the largest market segment for enterprise software. But prospective competitors have an eye on these companies, too. Therefore, in the future it will not be easy for SAP. The competitors that have seen sales lost to R/3's success will not be quick to admit defeat in the next round. "If SAP wants to hold the lead in the future, it has to set a fast development pace," comments Helmuth Gümbel, of the research group Strategy Partners in Munich.

On the question of which aspect of SAP's performance he appreciates most, *Computerwoche*'s Dieter Eckbauer, the longtime SAP observer and critic, answered: "Marketing." And SAP has no intention of slacking off here. To cover and extend its market position, as far as sales and technology are concerned, SAP increasingly has to focus on midsized companies. And its strategies are going to have to be slightly different from those it used to sell R/2.

For years, SAP's high prices had a deterrent effect on prospective midsized customers. "If you buy SAP, you pay the price for a luxury product," commented a German magazine. While no other software provider can offer enterprise software with comparable functionality for the planning, control, and analysis of business processes, R/3 users have had to pay a high price for implementation and maintenance because until 1996 the software package could only be implemented as a complete version—even when many program functions were not used. "It was as if the total contents of a mail-order catalog would be supplied as a compulsory delivery to a private household: ten large trucks with clothes, appliances, and consumer goods that nobody needs," criticized Friedrich Freiherr von Löffelholz, a professor at the University of Applied Sciences in Dortmund.

"Certainly we have still a lot to do in order to design our product so that it is simpler," admitted Hopp in March 1997 to the magazine *Focus*. On this occasion he also cited cases "in which we implemented R/3 within a few weeks." However, these were exceptions. For 60 percent of the R/3 installations that "went live" (SAP-speak) in spring 1997, implementation took *up to nine months;* most of the rest took even longer. But new computer-based methods should help to shorten the implementation phase. For example, Erhard Pohle, managing director of Ravensburger Spiele Verlag GmbH, looks pleased as he confirms: "We were able to use R/3 software after six months."

The advantage of SAP is that the success of R/3 has given them room to maneuver—to adjust their technology and service to the needs of mid-sized and small companies. The market success of a product like R/3 results in tremendous economies of scale. Therefore, SAP can invest without any difficulties in the further development of its software. One of the steps SAP has taken is to extend the range of industry-specific solutions offered. Currently SAP is focusing its worldwide marketing activities on sixteen industry sectors.

New sales strategies should accelerate SAP's market penetration at midsized companies. The decisive breakthrough in this context should be the new R/3 software architecture, implemented beginning in the fall of 1996.

Outstanding Financial Performance

The Federation of the European Business Press (UPEFE), an association of forty-two leading newspapers and magazines, honored SAP in 1996 as European Company of the Year. The performance of four thousand companies had been analyzed in terms of return on investment, return on equity, earnings per employee, and so on. The reasons for success? "I think we maintained the virtues of David [as opposed to Goliath]—that is to say, flexibility and agility," explains SAP cofounder Dietmar Hopp.

In September 1997 SAP received an AA rating and was ranked number one for the fifth consecutive year by the German monthly *Manager Magazin*, which analyzed the performance of German companies listed in the DAX (the German stock index).

In November of that year, the same magazine named SAP Company of the Year for the fourth time due to its financial performance and the advance in its stock price, and ranked it first among the top five hundred publicly held corporations in Europe.

Business Framework—A New Strategic R/3 System Architecture

In order not to jeopardize the investment companies have in existing R/3 installations, SAP began to reshape R/3 into a package of cross-sector and industry-specific components that can be implemented independently. In the spring of 1997 Hasso Plattner told the newsmagazine *Der Spiegel:* "Until one year ago, I insisted that a single software package could cover all business processes. Nowadays, I confess that I was wrong."

With this new approach, by the end of 1996, long before its competitors, SAP could already deliver dozens of special components with Internet functionality. This partially satisfies the call for object-oriented programming made by Karl Schmitz in 1995. However, the firm is under pressure to do more in this direction. Industry observer Bruce Richardson, from the United States firm AMR, comments: "We're seeing a real strong sense of impatience in the market."

The most important thing for the majority of customers is how quickly SAP software can be implemented. "Most companies want to implement the software within six months or in a shorter period. And competitors take advantage of this attitude."

As R/3 became more object-oriented, it was reorganized into three main cross-industry modules—accounting, logistics, and human resources—that can be implemented independently and supplemented by third-party stand-alone programs. On the basis of this new architecture, different components for specific business processes can be linked and delinked more easily.

Crucial for the integration into the total system are business application programming interfaces (BAPIs). In close cooperation with software market leader Microsoft, data exchange between business application programs of different software providers was standardized. Now third-party software providers can develop complementary components for R/3. "Even if you use standard software, you must have special components, for example, for retail selling, telephone selling, e-commerce, and direct sales," explains Hasso Plattner.

In the United States SAP's competitors were taken by surprise by the delivery of the first business framework components for the Internet use of SAP software. It was not the first time that SAP had pulled off such a coup. In August 1992 Dietmar Hopp and Hasso Plattner stunned first their own firm and then the United States market by suddenly advancing the debut of R/3 in the United States, which had been officially announced for January 1993. At a SAP user conference in Orlando, Florida, Plattner surprised the audience by announcing that the package could be bought immediately and would be delivered in six weeks; any mistakes in the English language of the program would be removed at the latest six weeks after delivery, at the expense of SAP. Enthusiastically the press paid tribute to the rare example of a software provider that introduced its product earlier than announced. And the first United States R/3 customer, the computer manufacturer Convex, signed a contract two weeks after the conference.

Main Competitors

Oracle

Oracle, the software giant from Redwood Shores, California, that was established in 1977 and was the number three software provider in the world in 1997, specializes in database programs, enterprise software, and multimedia software. It makes a good profit on its enterprise software—and it both cooperates with and competes against SAP. SAP primarily relies on Oracle's database system, and in 1996 80 percent of all R/3 installations in the United States were based on Oracle databases that could be operated under both Unix and Windows NT. In 1996 three thousand companies also used the enterprise software Oracle Applications—including Xerox, Kellogg, and Alcoa—despite the fact that not until 1995, three years after the debut of R/3 in the United States, could Oracle present a graphical user interface for its software. Since then, the firm has extended the functionality of its software and is regarded as a driving force in Internet software. "They're giving us hell in the United States, and we're going to do the same to them in Europe," said Raymond Lane, then president of worldwide operations at Oracle, in 1994. But these words seemed more bluster than anything else. In the spring of 1997 Hasso Plattner sneered in *Der Spiegel:* "We overtook Oracle, and today we are so far ahead of them that they cannot even see our taillights."

PeopleSoft

PeopleSoft, in Walnut Creek, California, was established in 1987 and started with application software for human resources (PeopleSoft HRMS) and payroll accounting. Now PeopleSoft is one of the fastest-growing United States firms and provides modules for production planning and sales, too. "SAP has been picking the low-hanging fruit the last few years with no real global competitors," said People-Soft founder Dave Duffield. "Now we're starting to see the competition." Like the cofounders of SAP, he is a former IBM man whose software idea met with resistance from his superiors. The human resources module of R/3 was for a long time regarded as one of the software's weaker components, and PeopleSoft took advantage of this—even in Germany. "Of all competitors, PeopleSoft is the one that fills us most with respect," comments Hasso Plattner. The firm, characterized by Plattner as a "fair and reliable competitor," startled SAP in 1996 as far as the Internet was concerned. "Now and then, you need such a competitor."

Baan

Baan was established in 1978 and started with client-server programs for production planning. The software package Baan IV (previously called Triton) is primarily used for production planning and control in the automotive industry as well as aircraft construction. Baan distinguished itself as SAP's most aggressive competitor and snatched prestigious orders away from SAP. The Dutch enterprise, which is listed on the NASDAQ, extended its product range, too. "The ability to configure and reconfigure the software has been a strength for us and a problem for SAP," notes Doug Sallen, United States manager of Baan. Says SAP's Hasso Plattner, "Baan was already a market leader for production planning software when we were busy with accounting and purchasing almost exclusively. Now we offer production planning software, too, and overtook Baan in its own market segment."

Additional Competitors

SAP must be aware of many additional software providers that are prospering, too. For example, the United States firms J. D. Edwards, in Denver, Colorado, and SSA/System Software Associates, in Chicago, Illinois, successfully provide enterprise software for the 64-bit computer system IBM AS/400, which is widespread in midsized companies.

Systems Integrators

Following SAP's example, since 1995 many software providers have opted to leave implementation of their software packages to influential consulting firms and special firms—the so-called systems integrators. Baan, for example, cooperates with IDS Scheer from Saarbrücken, who for years has had a close partnership with SAP, too.

Probably nowhere in the computer industry are the borders between competition and cooperation so fluid as in the market for enterprise software. The reason: Today no single provider is able to satisfy both the hardware and software requirements of corporate computing. Furthermore, in large installations—for example, at Siemens or Deutsche Telekom—very often software from competing providers is used simultaneously. Therefore, it pays to get one's production planning and logistics software implemented at a leading company. According to the domino principle, very often such a placement will result in follow-up orders from the suppliers of the first customer. Baan, for example, won first Boeing and later its supplier Contour Aerospace as customers.

Even when the signature is on the contract, the fight for the customer is not finished. It is really dangerous for a provider of enterprise software, particularly for the market leader, when a prestigious large-scale software package cannot be made to work properly for a customer. Such flops will be mercilessly exploited by competitors. The Walldorfers, too, are none too gentle about pointing out other companies' gaffes. For example, Hasso Plattner told *Der Spiegel*, "Take a look at how long it took Baan to implement at Boeing."

As a consequence of this fierce competition, even baseless rumors are created as a weapon. "In order to bring discredit upon SAP, even rumors about the supposed membership of board members in Scientology were launched," reported an analyst from Bayerische Vereinsbank about SAP in 1995. The Church of Scientology is looked upon with scorn in Germany, and there have been several notable confrontations between the group and the German government.

The handicap of almost all SAP's competitors is this: While they may offer integrated software for accounting, human resources, and production, mostly this is a patchwork of components bought or acquired within the scope of alliances with partner firms. Frequently, the limited usefulness of such software in an international context turns out to be these packages' most serious competitive disadvantage.

At SAP, however, foreign sales accounted for 81 percent of revenues in 1997. The internationally oriented firm nurtures internally multicultural management and cites it as a success factor. "When a German project manager leads a team of European, American, and Chinese employees, he should see to it that these employees know enough about the other cultures and have sufficient empathy," explains Wolfgang Fürniss, who is in charge of corporate relations. "Multicultural management is a conscious decision."

SAP has the competitive advantage of being able to offer R/3 in two dozen languages. The graphical user interface can be set not only to Cyrillic characters but also to Mandarin Chinese and Japanese kanji by means of a special double-byte technique. But R/3's multilingual attributes are not the only feature that accounts for its success internationally. For example, SAP industry-specific solutions in the chemical and oil industry can cover several time zones. By means of special selection menus the SAP software enables the sales manager of a global company to retrieve, for example, the order bookings for a certain date without having to worry about taking time and date differences into account—the software does it automatically.

An additional example: In some countries R/3 must allow for three-digit inflation values, fifteen-digit sales amounts, and—as in Brazil—three currencies (the real, an index currency, and the United States dollar). Moreover, SAP must monitor the legal and tax developments in the countries where R/3 is used in order to keep the software up to date.

SAP's Support Services

R/3 services are divided into three main areas: support, education, and consulting.

Support services handle software maintenance and troubleshooting. A three-tiered service concept has been established to offer customers the best possible service and support with quick response times. A worldwide, twenty-four-hour on-line service system (OSS) is available. Depending on the time, the support will be offered from Walldorf, California, or Singapore according to the motto "Follow the sun." More than 80 percent of SAP customers use remote connections and the OSS. By means of an automatic data download from the customer server, the customer's system is checked long before critical situations occur. In addition, with SAPNet, a new information and communication channel was established on the Internet. SAP operates four regional and thirty-five local support centers as well as six regional service centers. At the end of 1997 SAP had a service and support infrastructure of 2,400 employees (18 percent of the total workforce).

Education services focus on improving user qualifications and on continuous knowledge transfer. SAP operates sixty training centers worldwide.

Consulting services offer comprehensive support for R/3 implementation. In 1997 SAP employed 4,200 in-house consultants (33 percent of total employees), who were joined by some 30,000 consultants from external SAP partners.

As of December 1997 SAP had some 12,900 employees, all highly qualified professionals. This is made clear by the figure for sales per employee: $300,000.

In the fast-changing high-tech industry—where no provider is sure about its market share—a standstill in technology and service is regarded as a deadly sin. Therefore, in 1996 and 1997 SAP spent $393,000 (16 percent of sales) and $470,000 (14 percent of sales), respectively, on R & D.

"We regard the ability to innovate as a synonym for efficiency," explains Dietmar Hopp. But doubts about "whether competitors are better and could overtake us" are an integral part of the corporate culture of SAP, Hopp adds. "This uncertainty is one of our driving forces."

As an example, the SAP boss mentions the failure of the formerly successful German company Nixdorf, which was later taken over by Siemens. Founder Heinz Nixdorf "oriented his firm fully on sales and badly neglected product development," observes Hopp. And Hasso Plattner advises SAP employees to pay attention to a slogan of Andy Grove, Intel's CEO: "Only the paranoid survive."

Of this SAP was increasingly reminded in the United States by competitors, the trade press, and analysts in 1995 and 1996. The United States market for enterprise software is highly competitive, and the fear of an invasion by European software providers is strong. Gisella Wilson, a market analyst at IDC, warns: "They're simply hungrier." Mark Harwood, from the consulting firm Ernst & Young, pointed out that R/3 had become more than a product and called it a de facto standard, "like in the glory days of Big Blue."

But when the honeymoon was over, observers began to wonder

if SAP could keep up its success. "The world changed at IBM as hardware evolved into a commodity," wrote *Chemical Week*. "Might SAP, at the top of the heap, be headed for a similar fall?"

Top-down Approach in Selling

Anyone who wanted to find fault with SAP didn't have to wait long, because in the United States SAP forced its way into the market in a way that made it enemies in many companies' IT departments. "Basically, SAP has bypassed the IS department," concludes Alice H. Greene, a market analyst at Industry Directions in Newburyport, Massachusetts.

Instead of offering R/3 to the IT department, SAP went directly to the top, selling the software to CEOs and CFOs as an investment in infrastructure, using the slogan "A better return on information." Instead of selling a technology, comments Greene, "SAP has gone to the economic guys and convinced them that this software was going to change their businesses." SAP critic Dieter Eckbauer points out a possible consequence: "The board makes the decision, but the manager of the IT department has to carry the load." On the other hand, the otherwise quite critical technology consultant Karl Schmitz cites an additional secret of SAP's success: "Hopp, Plattner, and other board members are not above calling a customer's project manager if it will help. You have to admire this attitude."

Abroad, SAP partners often act as "door openers." Leading consulting firms like the Big Six (the six largest auditing firms of the world) as well as hardware manufacturers such as IBM, Bull, Siemens Nixdorf, Hewlett-Packard, DEC, and Sun worldwide steer the conversation around to R/3 on the executive floor. "SAP did a good job getting the Big Six [accounting] firms to sell its software," says IDC analyst Clare Gillan. Other SAP partners make it their business to adjust the software to the individual needs of the companies. This division of labor allows SAP to focus on software development and service as its core business. But it has also had negative conse-quences for customers. R/3 is reputed to be a "megabuck project" for large enterprises, and *Fortune* phrased it none too politely in 1995: "Consultants will camp out at your company."

Initiatives for Small and Midsized Companies

In 1994 Hasso Plattner affirmed that "we will serve the low-end mar-ket segment, too." But this was SAP's weak point for a long time. Nothing came of a "lite" version of R/3 that SAP announced in the United States under the name Heidelberg. The requirements of prospective clients turned out to be too varied for such a program. "Several of our smaller customers have the most complex business processes," explains Günther Tolkmit, head of technology marketing.

SAP began a marketing campaign in 1995 aimed at midsized companies, but at first it started slowly. In Germany, SAP entrusted sales of R/3 licenses to midsized enterprises with a sales revenue less than $150 million to twenty-nine R/3 "system houses"—value-added resellers (as of spring 1997). The system houses provide con-sulting, training, and service, too. A similar model of indirect selling started in the United States in 1996 with ten partners.

But in the magazine *Focus* Dietmar Hopp commented: "In the beginning, the system house partners acted hesitantly with respect to R/3, I suppose because they still tried to market their own old product."

The market is definitely there. Increasingly, midsized companies cannot afford to develop proprietary software for accounting, human resources, and logistics in-house or to outsource software development. Standard software seems to be more cost-effective and future-oriented. "Since we started using R/3, our data processing costs have been reduced considerably," notes Ulrich Masberg, CEO of Clouth Gummiwerke AG, in Cologne.

An additional advantage for SAP is that the plans for the European Currency Union and the Y2K problem put companies under pressure to invest in IT, to avoid the problems that obsolete software might cause. Moreover, increasing globalization leads the smaller suppliers of large R/3 customers to understand that they could benefit from using the same software as their multinational customers, as Hasso Plattner points out.

Chapter Five

Success in the United States— The Klaus Factor

The more complex the better. We Germans could never invent something as simple as Coca-Cola.

—HASSO PLATTNER

Without SAP, the German economy would break down," commented the United States consulting firm Gartner Group. And what about the United States? Without the enterprise software of SAP, the lights would go out there, too—literally.

If there were to be a breakdown of the SAP R/3 system, more than 13 million customers of Pacific Gas and Electric (PG&E) in central and northern California would suffer. The utility company, based in San Francisco, has used R/3 since 1994 for accounting, cost planning, materials and logistics management, project planning, human resources, and payroll accounting.

The implementation of SAP R/3 was finished in the three hundred PG&E branches in May 1996. Since then, for example, with a single transaction on the PC screen an order for material can be placed. With a few mouse clicks the required item can be transferred from the materials database to a purchase order form and a delivery date can be fixed. In 1996 more than 5,000 of the 21,000 employees of PG&E already used R/3 to retrieve—among other things—customer and budget data or to calculate the costs for the installation of a new transformer.

It takes two seconds, at most, for the required data from all sectors of the large company to appear on the PC screens in the utility's skyscraper on Beale Street in San Francisco. The computer system even works when there's a large amount of traffic on the PG&E network. "R/3 really gives our folks a powerful business tool to evaluate what it's going to cost to do anything in real time," raved John Danielson, IT manager of PG&E.

The software is "a dream for managers, who want to know what's what on the basis of organizational, financial, and production data," remarks Harry Tse, from the market research firm Yankee Group in Boston, Massachusetts. On the other side of the Charles River is another SAP user at which eight thousand jobs have been equipped with access to SAP R/3. "This client rates very high on the SAP customer list," says Dietmar Hopp. It is the Massachusetts Institute of Technology (MIT), perhaps the most famous high-tech university in the United States.

From MIT on the East Coast to Silicon Valley on the West Coast, all are in SAP's grip. "The United States is the key market for SAP," confirms Hasso Plattner. Meanwhile, the share price of SAP in Germany depends considerably on the exchange rate of the dollar. In 1997 SAP's sales revenue in the United States was $1.2 billion; that equals 35 percent of the company's total sales.

As of December 1997 SAP had 2,580 employees in the United States. New key accounts for SAP in 1996 were Motorola, Eastman Kodak, and Coca-Cola. And this is despite the fact that before 1993, most United States IT managers had not even heard of this software provider from Germany, even though SAP had been present in the United States via a subsidiary for five years.

The R/3 system was responsible for SAP's turnaround in the United States, catapulting the company's sales revenue from $59 million in 1992 to $1.2 billion in 1997. Before the managers of the leading United States software providers could correctly pronounce

SAP Sales Revenue in the United States

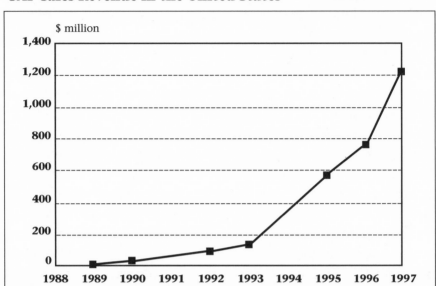

"SAP" at all, the outsider from Germany had already spread itself out in their home market, wrote the trade journal *Information Week*. Suddenly the R/3 CD-ROM was the hottest disk since Michael Jackson's *Thriller*.

Now the standard software from Wallendorf controls operations in almost all sectors of industry in the United States. For example, among SAP customers are Anheuser-Busch, Burger King, Coors, and Reebok.

"We penetrated a market that United States companies thought could be served only by United States companies," reflects Paul Wahl, who became chief of SAP America at the beginning of 1996 (and left the company in 1998). Almost every firm in the high-tech avant-garde of the United States computer industry stocked up on enterprise software from the Walldorfers, including Apple, Intel, and Microsoft.

"SAP's business applications have taken the Valley by storm," reported *Business Week*. The amazing rise of the German software provider in the United States was compared by *The Wall Street Journal* in the spring of 1995 with "a story that could have happened in Silicon Valley." In the first half of the 1990s hardly a day passed without another triumphant advance for SAP, and the United States media loved its success story.

Double Spearhead: Besier and Plattner

SAP decided to entrust the leading roles in its United States "software show" to Hasso Plattner and Klaus Besier. This filled the computer industry with enthusiasm. They were characterized as quick-witted gladiators from Germany aggressively entering the ring for the battle against domestic software heavyweights such as Dun & Bradstreet Software, Oracle, and Computer Associates. While the two of them appeared together on the cover of *Datamation* in March 1993—SAP cofounder, father of the SAP R/3 system, and part-time Californian Hasso Plattner, without necktie and wearing a sweater, and on his left, taller and in perfect business dress, the tanned Klaus Besier—watchful observers guessed that with two egos of this size in such close contact, the internal exchange of punches at SAP was a foregone conclusion.

The SAP marketing machine went full steam ahead, promising United States enterprises that they could optimize their business processes rapidly and flexibly as never before. SAP also assured companies groaning about clumsy mainframe systems that through R/3, relevant data could be made available anytime and anywhere with lightning speed. "If SAP delivers, then it is delivering what IT has been promising for a couple of decades," commented James A. Jones, managing director of the Information Management Forum, a peer organization in Atlanta. But he also pointed out that R/3 was being treated as if it were the "holy grail of IT."

For this software marvel, however, the price was steep. License costs were 50 percent higher in the United States than in Germany. SAP justified this by citing the considerably higher marketing expenditures that were necessary in the United States. But the follow-up costs—mostly unforeseen—could be tremendous, too. This PG&E soon found out. First they planned a budget of $35 million for the implementation of the new system. They "did a poor job of forecasting the budget," as the management of PG&E now admits. "We hadn't done a major system replacement in twenty-five years, and we didn't have the experience in predicting what a project like that would cost," explains Gordon R. Smith, senior vice president and CFO of PG&E.

Actually, the implementation costs were $70 million—twice as much as expected. For each dollar of software expenditure they spent ten dollars for implementation. In the end, "I was pleased that we were not spending $20 for every dollar," says Smith. Nevertheless, for the board of PG&E a retreat was out of the question. The old system consisted of sedate mainframe computers and a network of computers that were often more than twenty years old and had to be replaced.

The old system did not allow direct access to data that were needed for short-term optimization of current business transactions. Integration of data from different company sectors was simply out of the question. Anyone who needed a financial report gave the data processing center a call. Usually it then took several days until the right computer printout landed in the in box of the user. However, with R/3, a few mouse clicks meant that the report would appear on the PC screen in no time.

PG&E even writes reports for the United States Federal Energy Regulatory Commission by means of a specific R/3 module. Previously, preparing these reports required an expensive additional data input. Through a special-purpose software that was developed as an addition to R/3 by the German firm Heck & Partner, the reports are now largely automated. "We feel damn good having picked R/3," Smith says.

In 1996 the United States investment bank Salomon Brothers summarized the success of SAP in a report on the software industry in the United States: "From Nobody to the—Controversial—King Kong of the Applications Business." United States analysts and technical journalists quickly found out that SAP's success story had all the ingredients Americans loved: high technology, aggressive strategies, and big money. The interest in the smart entrepreneurs from Germany increased even further when aggressive competitors such as the young United States firm PeopleSoft and the Dutch company Baan attacked SAP's market, and people waited to see how the software giant would respond. After all, SAP had started out humbly in the United States in 1988, too.

Locational Choice

By United States standards, SAP's first branch in the United States was not a top address. Instead of leasing space in one of the dozens of mirrored glass buildings that flank Highway 101 through Silicon Valley, SAP America took rooms in a spacious but unimpressive building near the Philadelphia airport.

The austere—and soon too crowded—offices of SAP's first United States headquarters in the plain Airport Business Center were chosen because of their proximity to SAP's customers. In 1972 the U.K.-based chemical manufacturer ICI played an important role in SAP's start-up in Germany, and ICI America, SAP's first R/2 customer in the United States, was based in Wilmington, Delaware—near Philadelphia. DuPont, another R/2 customer, was based in Wilmington, too. The R/2 implementations in the chemical and oil industries formed the SAP bridgehead in the United States market. SAP implementations in Europe—as with ICI—had led to follow-up projects in the United States plants of the relevant industrial groups.

The new United States headquarters at first primarily served as support branch for R/2 users. In the first years of SAP's United States presence, the company relied on the strategies that had served them well in Europe: word-of-mouth advertising, a top-down sales approach (that is, pursuing client contacts at high levels), and support from pilot customers that demonstrate the use of R/2 in their industry. Even in 1990 Hasso Plattner justified SAP's decision to forgo a bigger advertising campaign: "An illustrious name in the customer file is worth a thousand times more than a very beautiful glossy brochure." It would be sufficient if SAP and R/2 were discussed at management conferences and specialized conventions. With a big key implementation "the market will be half conquered," the SAP cofounder self-confidently pointed out.

But the Walldorfers would learn that this approach was not appropriate for the United States. It is true that by 1989 Dow Chemical could be included in the customer file as SAP's thousandth customer worldwide. But in May 1989 SAP America counted seven customers. In the first two years after opening the United States branch, sales "visibly fell short of the expectations of the board," as it was announced to the press. In 1989 SAP's America's sales revenue was $7 million and in 1990 $16 million. With R/2, SAP could conquer only a small market niche, because the United States competitors were too strong.

By spring 1993 only 70 out of 1,800 R/2 customers were located in the United States. By then, for example, Dun & Bradstreet Software had 12,000 users of its mainframe business software. Dietmar Hopp admitted: "In the United States we will only succeed in business when we strongly expand our organization and sing the appropriate marketing tune for our product."

A further handicap for the newcomer from Germany was its name. "Before we went to the United States, we carefully considered whether we should use a different name," says SAP cofounder Klaus Tschira. "But in Europe the firm's name was already so widespread that we decided not to change it." But in the United States computer industry and at prospective customers the acronym SAP first triggered an amused shake of the head. The product name R/2 wasn't self-explanatory, but at least it was neutral. However, the mocking smiles over the name SAP meant that somebody should have informed the saps from Germany what *sap* means in English. "Since our start in the United States, whenever we enter new markets I consult a dictionary to see whether this word exists in the relevant language," Klaus Tschira says now with a rueful grin.

"It's hard to imagine that a company that named itself 'sap' might be worth paying attention to," wrote *Fortune*. At first the Walldorfers tried to neutralize the problem by adding three—meaningless—periods to their acronym, "S.A.P.," to force people to say it as three separate letters instead of the word *sap*. But soon that would no longer be necessary. In a very short while, United States companies would find out just what the German software company's new product, R/3, could do, and its name, as SAP manager Jeremy Coote put it, would then be "the only uncool attribute of our firm."

Klaus Besier

Through Klaus Besier, who managed SAP America from January 1993 to January 1996, the unknown company with the complex product suddenly got a face in the United States. "Besier, who was familiar with the United States market, added entrepreneurial spirit and a customer-oriented marketing strategy to a good product concept," commented *Handelsblatt*. "SAP came into the North American market when some of its competitors were transitioning product lines," recalls market analyst Clare Gillan, of IDC, "and SAP forged tight relations with the Big Six consulting firms and took off."

SAP's competitors underestimated, too, what impact the new information technology would have on the corporate structure of the users. Through its partner strategy SAP was prepared for it. The close partnership with big consulting firms such as Arthur Andersen & Co., with which SAP set up a joint venture, paid off. "When an SAP comes into the United States with a partner such as Andersen Consulting, the result is credibility," comments Gisella Wilson of IDC.

Dietmar Hopp explains further: "R/3 serves as a vehicle for lean production." The implementation was to be done by established United States partners who were familiar with the requirements of United States industry. Top managers used R/3 in order to reorganize their company through fundamental "business reengineering." "The United States market was ready for reengineering and client-server [computing]," explains Karl Newkirk, who is in charge of the worldwide SAP business of Andersen Consulting. "Bang! There was SAP."

Klaus Besier provided a good bang indeed. Blond, blue-eyed, and well turned out, Besier, who was born in Wiesbaden, Germany, in 1951, first came to the United States in July 1982 on behalf of Messer Griesheim, a subsidiary of Hoechst. After apprenticing with Messer Griesheim (as a clerk in this industrial company) and studying business administration back at the University of Applied Sciences in Berlin, Besier worked in Riyadh for a while. In the capital city of Saudi Arabia the urbane manager installed a bookkeeping and cost accounting computer system for a building contractor from Berlin. He then went back to the United States in order to install Nixdorf computer systems. In 1991 he joined SAP America as a marketing expert. "My advantage was not only that I was familiar with the country, but also that I was an expert in developing new business," remembers Besier. His boss at that time, Hans-Werner Hector, states: "Besier had a sure feel for picking up new customers. He knew all about United States marketing."

In February 1992 Hector came to the United States as CEO of SAP America. The SAP cofounder temporarily took over the function of president, too. Not everything was going according to the Walldorfers' plan, and, says Hector, "my first task was to convince the president at that time either to cooperate or to leave the company." He suggested giving Besier an equal hand in the company's affairs, but Jim Bensman, president of SAP America since 1989, refused. Consequently, Hector negotiated with Bensman about canceling his contract. "Suddenly, Bensman pulled a paper from his bag stating what severance pay he is entitled to—signed by Hopp and Plattner. I didn't know that."

After this incident, Hector bitterly complained about his cofounders leaving him in the lurch. "I was new in the United States, and that was—so to speak—my first experience in the country." A legal tug-of-war was the consequence. "We both got lawyers, and there was a tough struggle lasting several weeks." Hector's frustration increased. "If we are partners, then let's talk sense and don't try to trip each other up," he told his colleagues at the time.

Bensman eventually left SAP America, and in March 1992 Klaus Besier was promoted to chief operating officer and executive vice president of the United States subsidiary of SAP. In January 1993 he was appointed president of SAP America and thereby was also in charge of the SAP subsidiaries in Canada, Mexico, Australia, New Zealand, and Latin America, too. "Leadership qualities distinguished Besier," says Hector. "He held the team together. How he did business, how he led the employees, how he handled the press—he was sometimes on the brink of what could be allowed. With a subtle irony and aggression he fought against competitors—but always in a way that they couldn't go to court."

In a March 1993 article in the magazine *Datamation* Besier programmatically laid out his aggressive goal to "achieve in no time the biggest possible impact in the United States." At that moment only six customers in North America used R/3, so the story in the trade journal for IT managers was a prelude to a media campaign the likes of which the United States had not yet seen from a high-tech manufacturer from Germany. The message was that superior R/3 technology guaranteed safety for the future, exemplary integration of business processes, ability to be used internationally, and easy implementation. The R/3 system was backed by SAP's "German know-how." Besier arrogantly went on to proclaim, "That SAP only promises what we can deliver is what distinguishes us from other United States software providers."

Of course, this comment had to be considered in the context of a statement by the master of premature product announcements, Microsoft's Bill Gates, that his company would cooperate with the German software provider in order to adapt R/3 to the successful network operating system Windows NT. A well-known customer from the media industry, the daily newspaper *Seattle Times*, increased the credibility of SAP's $2 million campaign.

The *Times* had been using the mainframe software of Dun & Bradstreet (DBS) for accounting. When they decided to convert the system to a client-server network, the *Seattle Times* chose R/3 instead of DBS software. The managers justified their decision this way, according to Laurie Stanton, the newspaper's financial accounting manager: "From a financial standpoint they met what we were looking for. We also knew that anything else we added would be fully integrated."

Datamation, which has a reputation for being critical, confirmed that the *Times* had a good experience in implementing R/3. After a test of only two weeks, the *Seattle Times*—supported by consultants from ICS Deloitte—converted its accounting from mainframe computing to a decentralized client-server architecture with R/3. To operate the old system as backup would have doubled the workload, for example at data input, so they decided to switch with no backup. If the experiment had failed, there would have been no turning back. But as *Datamation* wrote: "The *Seattle Times* took only 88 days to prove wrong the critics who say it takes eons and costs megabucks to move to R/3."

The real costs for the *Seattle Times*, however, would become apparent three years later. At the time, though, its positive experience resulted in dozens of enthusiastic referrals for SAP.

Market Entry: Double Strategy

SAP managed its breakthrough in the United States market through a double strategy: On one hand, SAP tried hard to convince customers in the oil, chemical, and pharmaceutical industries of the advantages of R/3. Simultaneously, SAP focused on winning computer manufacturers and software providers as customers—or as partners. If they implemented the software from Germany, they would become trendsetters for other sectors of industry, too.

The sales bonus scheme that Besier and Hector developed together served as an important lubricant for the SAP sales organization. They abolished the previous upper limit of $140,000 for sales commissions. *Business Week* wrote: "Some top German executives still flinch when they hear that a salesperson can earn more than they do"—up to $2 million a year. "First, Plattner planned to do it on the West Coast. But we had already decided to do it for the whole country," recalls Hans-Werner Hector. "When Hopp heard about it, he nearly bit my head off."

The first large order for R/3 was placed by Chevron, based in San Ramon, near San Francisco. The leading oil company in the United States ordered a software package that included financial accounting (FI), controlling (CO), asset management (AM), and materials management (MM). This first key account was served by SAP experts from the West Coast. In the beginning of 1991 SAP established its second United States office in Redwood City, in the northern part of Silicon Valley. There, twelve employees served customers such as Hitachi and Nestlé.

The R/3 implementation at Chevron became the acid test in a market where only the powerful predecessor product R/2 seemed to stand out. SAP met with skepticism when it recommended for Chevron a client-server architecture that at first glance seemed to be more suitable for midsized enterprises. This skepticism was cleared up in negotiations by painful concessions. Plattner says: "We had to pay through the nose in this Chevron implementation." But when the software proved to work for Chevron and other companies became aware that standard software for client-server computing with a comparable degree of integration was not yet available from SAP's competitors, SAP's sales soared. "We gave our competitors such a shock that they were frozen for three years," gloats Plattner. In 1993 the volume of new orders trebled, to $113 million, and SAP quickly established additional branch offices in the United States. Later Raymond Lane, a member of the Oracle board, admitted that SAP had caught his company with its "pants down." This Oracle manager and his boss, Larry Ellison, could almost watch from their windows as SAP settled quite comfortably into their neighborhood in California, soon opening their first development center outside of Germany.

The Dutch competitor Baan had opened a branch in Menlo Park, only a few miles south. "All our competitors were based in the

United States or settled there," says Plattner. "They were bunched up. It was right not only to establish a sales organization, but to set up a development center, too. Meanwhile, all this talk about globalization—we had been in the lead."

Technological evolutions and revolutions frequently emerge in Silicon Valley. That this is true was made clear to the Walldorfers quite soon after moving in.

At first, the renaissance of the valley announced itself only through small things. Young IT professionals brought into the office a glossy magazine that recently had started up in San Francisco. Its title was *Wired*. E-mail addresses were displayed on the cars of young programmers. On the six-lane expressways billboards advertising radio stations or airlines began to add the addresses of these companies' Web sites. At first experienced IT professionals might have dismissed this as a passing trend, but soon they realized that the future of many companies—including SAP—would hinge on their ability to work with the Internet.

Foster City has a population of more than thirty thousand—about double the population of Walldorf. The town is situated in the marshland of San Mateo County, on San Francisco Bay. IT professionals from Germany or SAP customers who know the SAP headquarters in Walldorf see in the scenery of the bayside community a strong contrast to the historic buildings of Walldorf.

Foster City, advertised as "California's first planned community," is a town from the drawing board and the computer. It is proud of that. The first residential buildings were not constructed until 1963. Today, Foster City, with its twelve residential enclaves sharing space with artificial lakes, is primarily a bedroom community for commuters, most of whom work in San Francisco, to the north, or in San Jose, an hour south.

There is no real main street in Foster City. Anyone looking for a center would find himself at an office tower looming twenty floors over a spacious ensemble of shopping centers, parking garages, and uniform row houses.

While the rest of the town seems to be completely deserted during the day, the elevators in the office tower are buzzing. Many of the passengers are IT professionals. Microsoft rents offices in the building, as does the Japanese software group that owns the publishing company Ziff-Davis, and also the leading United States computer show, Comdex. The sixteenth floor of the tower accommodates SAP Technology, Inc.—a subsidiary of SAP America.

The SAP development center in Foster City soon evolved into the second headquarters of the rapidly growing market leader for enterprise software. In the air-conditioned "cybertower" Walldorf seems to be far away—and then again not: German is frequently heard in the elevators there.

Hasso Plattner spends a third of his time in California. "In Silicon Valley beats the heart of technological innovations," enthuses Plattner. And SAP was willing to spend money on such innovations. When SAP took over market leadership for client-server applications in the United States, it already spent more for R & D than its five biggest competitors put together. Market analysts at IDC and other firms attentively watched, seeing that SAP apparently was not yet satisfied with its success in the United States. SAP had recognized how important it was to keep moving and never to rest on past successes.

"The main objective in establishing the development center had been to be connected with our most important business partners as closely as possible and to be integrated into the technology world," explains Plattner. They succeeded, as evidenced by a headline from *Business Week:* "America's Latest Software Success Story Is German." The article went on to say that SAP's U.S. client list "reads like a Who's Who of Silicon Valley."

At first, Klaus Besier planned to take things slowly. But the response SAP got to R/3 from high-tech enterprises right from the beginning caused the board in Walldorf to change its mind and move ahead faster. SAP could rely on the "early adopters" in ready-to-experiment northern California—courageous initial users who signed up to implement a software system that had not yet been tested for very long.

Mostly, such companies' buying decisions were influenced by the strategic advantage that they expected from the software's high degree of integration. A typical example is the software provider Autodesk, which specializes in software for design and construction. After implementation of R/3, Autodesk developed from a SAP customer into a SAP partner in the "Golden Gate Project," in which R/3 modules are customized for the software industry. "If we are short of inventory in Singapore, we can ship the product from the United States and we won't lose the order," explains Bill Kredel, IT manager of Autodesk, in describing the impact of R/3. For Autodesk, based in San Rafael, the implementation of R/3 paid off in only six months thanks to the need to keep less stock on hand.

Before the implementation of R/3, the company had struggled with twenty thousand internal article codes—for only forty products total. By means of R/3, the number could be reduced to sixteen hundred. The technical standardization of the system benefited customers, too. The time between placing an order and shipment previously had been two weeks. After replacing the mainframe system and implementing R/3, the throughput time amounts to twenty-four hours.

In a climate where mainframe software still operated with text-oriented screen masks, R/3's new graphical user interface appealed to managers who were used to Apple's or Microsoft's interfaces. The front end was clearly important. Nevertheless, SAP apparently did not take great trouble with its interface. Industry experts and users criticized the interface for being different—for example, in terms of the icons—from the de facto standard, Windows. However, SAP brushed aside these comments. After all, it still was the first supplier of such a product. "You can criticize that we didn't make all the decorations and borders like Microsoft. But the crucial fact is that it looked like Windows," Hasso Plattner says.

Hasso Plattner

Like Besier, Hasso Plattner had a nose for what was important in the United States market. So, for example, the user conference—called Sapphire—that SAP organized for the first time in 1990 in the United States was turned into a magnificent event that now attracts thousands of SAP experts every year. On this occasion, not only software is on the agenda. Past guest speakers have included the futurologist Alvin Toffler, the late publisher Malcolm Forbes, Apollo 13 commander James Lovell, and Microsoft boss Bill Gates.

At the Sapphire user conference at Disney World in 1994, 4,400 IT professionals from thirty-one countries saw there the most unusual lecture that an ambassador of the German high-tech industry has ever given abroad. An R/3 technology update was on the agenda, and the audience resignedly waited for the usual overhead transparencies about ABAP/4 and business workflow. But when it was time, artificial fog welled up and glaring lights flashed through the darkened hall. Then loud chords roared from the stage loudspeakers. The shadowy figure of a man with an electric guitar in hand slowly emerged from the fog. It was Mr. R/3 himself—Hasso Plattner, at that time deputy CEO of SAP AG. "I always wanted to know what it would be like to play in front of several thousand people," Plattner said later.

For Americans, the self-made billionaire personifies a new type of German entrepreneur. Also, the sports spirit of the SAP cofounder made him popular, especially in competition-minded Silicon Valley. Plattner made headlines not only with R/3 but also as a yachtsman. He customized his powerful racing yacht *Morning Glory* with state-of-the-art computers and the latest technology from California ship designers and builders. "Dr. Plattner also wanted the best consultants on our team, because today's computer programs . . . are highly sophisticated and demand no less than experts to achieve the best results," says John Reichel, head of Reichel/Pugh Yacht Design in San Diego.

The eighty-foot racing yacht was built in record time. It took only seven months until the boat was finished at the McConaghy Yacht Shipyard in Sydney, Australia. Simulation programs had been developed particularly for this project, and eighty hours of machine time was booked on a Cray supercomputer. "It was the most intensive study on the efficiency of yachts ever made," explains Plattner. It attracted attention in Silicon Valley not only because of its technology and cost but because another resident software mogul sailed his own seventy-eight-foot yacht, *Sayonara,* in the same class: Larry Ellison, of the software giant Oracle.

When in October 1996 at the Kenwood Cup off Hawaii Plattner's carbon-fiber-reinforced mast broke, regatta winner Ellison could not resist issuing an official Oracle publication: "*Morning Glory,* owned by Oracle competitor SAP CEO Hasso Plattner of Germany, did not compete due to a mast break which occurred during the second day of the race. Prior to *Morning Glory's* architectural woes, the 80-foot yacht and the *Sayonara* competed three times, the *Sayonara* prevailing twice and the *Morning Glory* once."

On the other hand, the sailing comradeship of the software rivals—who are also partners in the database sector—technologically pays off for SAP, says Plattner. "When I needed a copy of a NT database that was not yet released by Oracle, nobody would hand it over. I called Larry. Twenty minutes later I had a tape with the Oracle database."

Plattner's greatest hour on the high seas came in the Hobart Sydney Regatta from New Zealand to Australia in December 1996. Plattner was the winner in record time (Ellison was not present). Even the newsmagazine *Der Spiegel* paid tribute to Plattner's victory in a detailed article. It reported that a sophisticated SAP program—the ABAP/4 Sailing Performance Monitor—that had been developed by Plattner supported the twenty-man crew, optimizing the yacht's speed through computerized analysis of wind and waves. SAP could not have wished for better advertising for its software.

Like Plattner with his yacht, after the breakthrough of R/3 in the United States, SAP was regarded as an example of an aggressive entrepreneurial sport spirit that was new for Europe. Not overlooked was the irony that the idea for standard software originally had been developed by IBM, but was not pursued by the mother of all computer manufacturers and instead had been turned into cash by the clever SAP people. So the market analysts in the United States regarded it as a victory for SAP when, twenty-two years later, Big Blue had to order its standard business software from its former employees at the office in Mannheim.

Still, in the spring of 1994, IBM took over the French company CGI Informatique, which specialized in accounting software. To industry experts, this step seemed to be a sure sign that a rival product to R/3 was planned. But this project soon proved to be the last, desperate effort by Big Blue to avoid acknowledging the superiority of SAP. In November 1994 SAP announced the biggest order in company history: IBM had decided to use R/3 in purchasing, materials management, and order processing.

After this news, the share price of SAP jumped to a record level of $648.15, and market capitalization increased to more than $6.173 billion. United States industry experts remembered on this occasion how Big Blue had let the SAP founders leave with their concept for standard software. "IBM hasn't made such a smart move since Tom Watson Sr. turned down the chance to buy the patents for the Xerox machine," chortled *Information Week*.

The Boeing Flop

In trying to win the aircraft manufacturer Boeing as a customer, SAP was brought back to reality in the highly competitive United States market. Boeing is the world's largest private data processor—its data processing department has about ten thousand employees. But in August 1994 Boeing decided to use Triton software from the Dutch software provider Baan.

After the steep rise of SAP in the United States, this "crash landing" was all the more visible, wrote *Wirtschaftswoche*. They quoted a

Boeing spokesperson: "Due to design errors, it would have taken ten months until we could have processed the first order with R/3." That might have given the impression that an already ongoing SAP implementation had been broken off. Actually, that was not the case.

Losing such a large order made it unmistakably clear to the Walldorfers that their competitors would no longer just sit back and watch SAP take over the United States market. SAP lost the Boeing order because it could not mobilize adequate resources due to the terrific growth of the preceding months. SAP experts who were needed for the Boeing project—among other things—were tied up with R/3 evaluations at two other well-known industry giants, Intel and Microsoft. While SAP had its hands full, Baan could take advantage of this opportunity, and Jan Baan rejoiced: "Boeing's decision on Baan for us is a confirmation that we are on the right track with our products and services."

At the end of 1993 Boeing Commercial Airplane Group (BCAG) had considered implementing R/3 for production planning and supply chain management. Boeing needed a software that would allow the production resources in airplane manufacturing to be controlled more effectively—for example, in purchase order processing, materials and logistics planning, and production planning. For instance, Boeing wanted to be able to transmit customers' specific equipment requirements concerning floor coverings, seat models, appliances for the galley, lavatory equipment, and the like directly via computer to the design department.

Boeing asked the leading software providers in this area for test installations in order to evaluate their performance for this type of aircraft construction. More than a dozen SAP experts were sent to Reston, near Seattle, in order to configure R/3. But the test installation was more difficult than expected, and SAP asked for more time to develop an operational model of the system and present it to a panel of fifty experts. But Boeing would not agree to a postponement. Boeing apparently saw this request as an "affront," reported Plattner later. The consequence was that SAP withdrew from the bidding for the prestigious large order. Later, Dietmar Hopp tried to put the retreat in a better light: "We thought it best to turn down customers when we cannot offer what they ask for."

If the Walldorfers had hoped to let the Boeing fiasco silently drop out of sight, they had reckoned without Jan Baan. The hungry Baan could not have dreamed up a better occasion for publicity in the United States. The contract from Boeing was, so to speak, Baan's admission ticket for additional key accounts in the United States. Simultaneously, Baan's success demonstrated that apparently there was a European alternative to SAP that should be taken seriously.

Oliver Elser, the marketing boss of Baan in Germany, bragged: "Through the super reference it became known worldwide that we can serve large enterprises, too." Shortly afterward, Baan announced a large contract with Canadian Northern Telecom. And Daimler-Benz decided on Baan in the spring of 1995 when it selected enterprise software for a new car plant in Tuscaloosa (though Daimler-Benz used R/3 elsewhere). But it was not only Baan that SAP had to worry about. In the fall of 1994 in Germany—in SAP's home market—PeopleSoft did business with Siemens AG, SAP's biggest customer. Hopp commented later: "We have learned to be afraid of our competitors and to acknowledge them."

Siemens declared that SAP would remain their most important software provider. But for HR management they preferred PeopleSoft, with whom they signed a $2.5 million contract, "because several of our United States subsidiaries already used HR software from PeopleSoft." Michael Pfister, press spokesman for SAP, commented: "This example shows that we are not the monopolist we are often regarded as."

When the news of such setbacks leaked out, the Walldorfers always overreacted. Dietmar Hopp bitterly complained: "Our Dutch competitor Baan attacks SAP with special unfairness." Hopp especially overreacted to the inquiries of journalists. "In the United States, sixty-five high-tech firms are our customers: Microsoft, IBM, Hewlett-Packard, DEC, Compaq, Apple, and so on. Do you really think that these companies buy only obsolete software?"

Grumbling about SAP seemed to become the media's new sport in Germany, and SAP lashed back. In *Computer Zeitung* Dietmar

Hopp complained: "I find it strange that cheers break out in the press when one of our competitors gets an order we tried to get, too." The CEO of SAP gave another opinion in the weekly *Die Woche*: "Recently, all sorts of things are taken against us in order to tread on our toes." As an example, he mentioned media reports that connected SAP with Scientology. Then the SAP boss mourned: "It seems to be a typical German characteristic to speak ill of somebody who gets somewhere." SAP even claimed that the bad press was launched by competitors.

It is true that the press in Germany at that time very rarely sang SAP's praises about its success in the United States. But there is no evidence of any kind of concerted campaign against SAP. However, the SAP boss feared—not without good reason—that such reports could multiply and have a detrimental effect on the share price. After all, United States trade magazines had picked up a story in *Wirtschaftswoche* in March 1995 whose theme was: "SAP is too rigid, too expensive, too powerful."

Light and Shadow

Setbacks like Boeing and Daimler-Benz did not mean a drop in SAP's United States business. SAP succeeded in increasing the sales revenue of SAP America in 1995 by 51 percent. Nevertheless, SAP's "honeymoon" with journalists and analysts seemed to be over in the United States, too.

SAP, which had entered the United States market as an underdog, became the market leader there in record time. In this position, SAP had to put up with critical questions from United States market analysts. "For one season we had been the child of surprise," Paul Wahl says of the change of the climate. "The United States market absolutely is the toughest we have. It was obvious that they would attack us as market leader quite differently. Who would have been interested in a story about what we do right?"

SAP's record in the United States is not unblemished:

- **PG&E** The implementation costs were twice as high as estimated. But who can blame SAP for this failure?
- ***Seattle Times*** While they implemented R/3 in the record time of three months, they initially installed a high-end server—an IBM RS/6000—to serve fifty users with 486 and Pentium PCs. This was more than the server could handle. Therefore, they had to buy two additional IBM servers. The extension and the new configuration of the system were supported by system consultants of the United States IBM/SAP Competency Center. But unlike the first implementation of R/3, there was only very ambiguous praise from the *Seattle Times* after finishing the expensive reconditioning in 1995, when IT manager Michael Topp said of the consultants: "They were all very knowledgable, and they didn't quit until all problems were solved."
- **Top-down Sales Approach** As in Germany, in the United States the SAP sales representatives made no secret of the fact that they would not waste their time on IT managers. Instead, they preferred to go to the board of directors right away. IT managers who had had influence in the past saw themselves demoted to technicians in reengineering experiments. If the SAP implementation failed, they were the ones left holding the bag. And if it succeeded, they risked watching their staff, now with R/3 experience, being hired by the consulting firm who did the implementation.

Weaknesses of SAP R/3

It quickly became common knowledge in the United States that the implementation of R/3 very often required lengthy implementation periods, high expenditures for external system consultants, and more money spent on training system users. When competitors awakened from their initial shock, they did not neglect to point out this situation. In their advertising, Baan and Oracle drew attention to the fact that the ratio of software license fees to implementation costs for their products was about 1:2. In contrast, for SAP it was between 1:5 and 1:10. Again, the truth of the claim could not be denied, so in February 1995 Dietmar Hopp said, "R/3 is in its functionality so superior that our focus now must be to implement it more cost-effectively."

Strengths of SAP R/3

In the United States market R/3 developed enormous momentum. The Gartner Group likened R/3 to an avalanche.

The hardware manufacturers and software providers as well as the consulting and training firms involved with SAP experienced a boom. But anyone who wanted to ride the R/3 wave—as user, hardware manufacturer, software provider, system consultant, or analyst—was dependent on the goodwill of the Walldorfers. Therefore, the ambivalence about SAP increased. "I need them more than they need me," moaned Richard Luciano, who was in charge of the connection to SAP at DEC. While SAP safeguarded the market that was so profitable for all parties involved, deviating from the SAP course was punished harshly—as hardware partner DEC found out.

DEC managers were shocked when SAP severely punished what the DEC people saw as an insignificant insubordination. DEC had sold new database software to SAP competitor Oracle and on top of that agreed on a joint marketing initiative. It was not long before the DEC managers realized that they were no longer being asked to participate in SAP projects. The crisis was settled only when Vincenzo Damiani, who was a member of the DEC board and in charge of worldwide sales, apologized to Klaus Besier. Now and then the partners were "reminded" what it meant to mess with Klaus, wrote *PC Week.*

Hints of arrogance in the United States sales organization caused concern in Walldorf. Libby Wright, the IT manager of National Instruments in Austin, Texas, described SAP's attitude as "arrogant," recalling SAP asking for $1 million per module or to "forget it."

Costs of R/3 Implementation

United States experts estimated that an admission ticket into the R/3 world costs, on average, at least $4 million. The greatest part of this went for implementation and training. How the implementation could be simplified was demonstrated by Hasso Plattner for the first time at the Sapphire user conference in August 1995. Six thousand people from forty-six countries attended this conference.

The marketing message was: "Nothing simpler than R/3." Plattner amazed the audience by demonstrating the latest version of the highly complex and memory-hungry R/3 release 3.0 on a notebook PC. The trick was to preinstall the complete system but deactivate those modules the customer was not expected to use. If if turned out that any deactivated module would in fact be needed, it could be activated on the spot. Finally, the customized configuration could be transferred into the computer system of the customer. This was presented to the SAP community as the future of R/3, a way to considerably accelerate the implementation and fine-tuning of the software.

Bottleneck: SAP Consultants for System Implementation

But who should configure the R/3 system? The technical trick just described might reduce the implementation costs. But another reason implementation costs were so high was an acute shortage of qualified SAP system consultants. As a result of the boom in standard software, the demand for R/3 consultants had exploded in the United States market. Meanwhile, the fees they charged reached a staggering level.

"We didn't realize it would cost this much," complained an IT manager at the United States arms manufacturer Remington. And as the firm found out, the ability to pay was not enough: "We had wanted to schedule SAP training. But they're all booked up."

Large enterprises desperately looked for SAP consultants and were willing to pay top rates. Want ads appeared everywhere—in the *Wall Street Journal*, on the Internet. The gold-digger mentality increasingly made itself felt in the SAP world. High fees that could be easily earned attracted software "soldiers of fortune" in droves. "Minimal experience with the system can lead to a very lucrative job," said one ad.

The SAP management knew that in order to safeguard their United States business they had to provide enough qualified R/3 experts, and do it quickly. When R/3 first came onto the United States market, experts from SAP supported customers in system implementation, but the extent of the boom made this solution unworkable now. "There were not enough people to do consulting," recalls Alexander Ott, who has since left the company to join Siebel Systems, one of SAP's fiercest competitors. "It was ludicrous to hire three thousand people, so we trained partners." Through this measure SAP could safeguard R/3's success without annoying its alliance partners in the service sector by developing a huge consulting force of its own to compete with theirs.

Strategic Alliances

While SAP did not wish to irritate its alliance partners, the company that had developed R/3 still set the rules, and it paid to comply with these rules. Klaus Besier boasted: "We have seven hundred registered who want to partner with us." The partner strategy was no charity event—the partners, for example, had to pay for booths at marketing events such as the Sapphire user conference—but they went along. At the end of 1994 the leading consulting partners announced that they would additionally assign several thousand of their own employees to R/3 implementation. These leading consulting partners were Andersen Consulting, Price Waterhouse, KPMG, Ernst & Young, Coopers & Lybrand, ICS-Deloitte, IBM, Cap Gemini America, and Origin.

Moreover, SAP America established a training academy, with

training centers in Dallas, Texas, and Toronto, Ontario, Canada. The training program covered aspects such as software architecture, R/3 modules, project management, and methods of systems integration.

Simultaneously, SAP looked for academic recruits. They extended and intensified their cooperation with universities. "The introduction of R/3-related courses in the curricula of reputable technical universities will contribute to a more widespread basis of knowledge about the client-server technology," announced SAP in the spring of 1995.

In late 1995 SAP had twenty-five branch offices in North America. The number of training centers increased to sixty. Earlier that year Price Waterhouse had opened an international training center in Philadelphia also. By then the partner firms employed five thousand R/2 and R/3 consultants.

The business press praised the foresighted partner strategy of SAP, but would it really work? Could it bridge the consultants gap?

It seemed that these efforts weren't enough. At a software conference run by Andersen Consulting in August 1995, SAP customers complained publicly that SAP was neglecting service due to its rapid growth. The next year *Chemical Week*, the trade magazine for the chemical industry in the United States, analyzed the position of SAP in the United States and concluded, "SAP's Achilles' heel, however, may be software installers."

"If somebody's looking for an R/3 consultant with three years of experience, there are not too many around because we just launched the product three years ago," Klaus Besier replied huffily, countering an inquiry about the tiresome problem of a "shortage of SAP implementation specialists" in December 1995. SAP managers continually rejected criticism and referred instead to the indisputable success of the partner strategy in the United States market. Actually, it was more successful than the company really wanted, since the SAP model was regarded as so exemplary that it was quickly adopted by SAP's United States competitors.

"The need to partner is becoming increasingly clear to financial application vendors, particularly those that find themselves up against SAP," wrote *Software Magazine*. Competitors such as DBS, PeopleSoft, Baan, and Oracle now formed strategic alliances with consulting firms. System integrators would play a key role in the success of the large providers of enterprise software, according to forecasts of the market research firm IDC in 1995. Due to the complexity of client-server computing, software providers must offer an adequate support for implementation, found IDC. As a result, the demand for experienced system consultants increased further.

Things may change, however. Some United States computer experts are of the opinion that the complicated client-server computing model may soon end up in the computer museum. The comparatively simpler Internet technology might indeed be its successor.

Klaus Besier's Vision

In any case, Klaus Besier was convinced by December 1995 that the future of the software business lay in the Internet, where there are no platform borders. There the data traffic is controlled by the TCP/IP transmission protocol, which can connect a primitive PC with state-of-the-art Unix servers or, in turn, these with an IBM mainframe computer. Besier saw, as he said later, "an opportunity here to be part of a new wave of technology that changes the way people conduct business and communicate."

Until 1994 the Internet was regarded as the domain of universities, large research institutes, and high-tech firms, which had developed the decentralized system with the United States Army and then adopted it in order to extend it for scientific and economic use. Now a study by the market research firm Input pointed out the direction in which Silicon Valley was headed: The expenditures of companies for Internet technology had trebled to $12 billion between 1994 and 1995.

One main reason for the investment in Internet technology was that client-server computing had turned out not to be as cost-effective as originally expected. This applied not only to the use of standard enterprise software such as R/3 but also to document management systems and companywide e-mail systems. Such "open" systems mean tremendous expenditures for software maintenance. In large enterprises with several thousand networked servers, workstations, and PCs, the update of client software was a large project that could occupy the system experts for weeks. In contrast, network-centered data processing increasingly appeared to be a less-expensive alternative. In such a system, the current software version would be available on the intranet or from the software provider via the Internet. With a mouse click users could download and install the required software on their PC.

Larry Ellison, CEO of SAP's competitor Oracle, saw this as a promising possibility, too. Oracle was the first large software provider to offer its management programs for downloading via the Internet.

CNN, the *New York Times*, and *Wired,* among others, reported that e-commerce would be boosted by the new technologies. But when Klaus Besier wanted to develop a Web site in 1995, "the Walldorfers didn't have the faintest idea of what a home page was"—or at least, this was how he expressed it later, after leaving SAP.

Did SAP miss a promising market, as such statements would indicate? On the other hand, Klaus was notorious for making a big noise about his own contributions to the success of SAP in the United States and downplaying others' roles. At the time, Hans-Werner Hector told his colleagues: "Klaus is incredibly good, but incredibly arrogant, too. He thinks that he's invaluable to SAP. We'll have to keep a close watch on him."

Even outside observers noticed that Besier did not like adapting to the corporate culture of SAP. And in contrast to the prevailing outlook at Walldorf, which was basically committed to discretion, Besier was exceptionally outspoken, especially with the press, to which he commented on how he thought the "slow Germans" at home should be treated. *Business Week* wrote in August 1994, the same month in which Besier pulled out of the bidding for the Boeing contract: "Besier clearly likes to shake things up back in Walldorf. . . . When he penciled in $2 million for advertising as part of his $6 million budget for the U.S. launch of R/3, SAP's board balked. Besier spent it anyway—and turned in sales $2 million above the company's forecast." The magazine quoted Besier: "I prefer to beg for forgiveness than for permission." But such demonstrations of independence at the top of their United States subsidiary were something the board could not tolerate. They let him know that the course would still be decided in Walldorf.

After his withdrawal from the SAP board in May 1996, Hector complained that Besier had tried to play the cofounders off against each other. "At first, he hung on to Plattner when he figured out that Plattner didn't tell me everything," says Hector, who represented the SAP board in Philadelphia until the spring of 1995. "Afterward, he got close to Hopp when he realized that Plattner didn't tell Hopp everything." Hector notes that the cofounders increasingly became estranged from one another. "He took advantage of things that hadn't been a problem with us in the past." Kagermann dryly comments that corporate politics were not one of Besier's shortcomings. But at the same time, the gap between Hans-Werner Hector and his cofounders grew.

Things between Besier and Plattner entered a state of crisis when the launch of R/3 in the United States revealed unforeseen problems. Specific program functions that originally had been developed for the German version failed in the United States version due to translation mistakes. Criticism from Walldorf was received poorly by Besier, who overreacted.

Someone who was there at the time recalls: "Besier and Plattner didn't know the first thing about management, that he needed to take care of development and ensure that the products worked in the United States, too." They had arguments on personnel affairs as well. Besier (and Walldorf board members) confirms that there were loud arguments, mainly between himself and Plattner, and mentions frustrations about "several disputes with Plattner."

At that time a wave of high-tech start-ups was occurring all over the United States, not just in Silicon Valley. For example, Business@Web in Watertown, Massachusetts, was regarded as a promising venture—the business magazine *Upside* counted this firm among the top fifty Internet-related start-ups in the United States. One of the founders of the company was MIT professor John Donovan, who also founded the consulting firm Cambridge Technology Group.

His idea was to develop business software for the Internet that consists of compact, multipurpose software components (called objects). Such objects can be combined to form novel applications. James Nondorf, another of the founders of Business@Web, announced in *Upside* magazine: "We could be on every desktop five years from now." Klaus Besier became aware of this new firm, too. He remembers discussing the potential of the new technologies and their economic impact with John Donovan late into the night.

Marc Andreessen was another high-tech entrepreneur regarded as a shining example of the new generation. Andreessen had developed the browser Mosaic at the National Center for Supercomputer Applications at the University of Illinois, providing millions of PC users with a window on the Internet. With Jim Clark, the founder of Silicon Graphics, Andreessen set up in 1994 a company in Palo Alto that developed this Internet software further for commercial use. The result was Netscape Navigator, which was launched at the end of that year and became the most widely used application for PCs. When Netscape Communications went public in August 1995, the share price increased by 200 percent over the initial offering in one day—and Andreessen became a millionaire overnight.

United States investors already held 13 to 14 percent of SAP's shares. Would the whiz kids from Walldorf go public in the United States, too? This was the question increasingly asked by United States journalists and analysts. But in Germany, the board of SAP was immune to the stock exchange fever hitting the United States high-tech industry; their standard answer was "We have no need for more funding." But Besier had a different view, and again he made the disagreement public.

In the high-tech investment magazine *Red Herring* Besier explained that the SAP board was balking at the required quarterly disclosures needed if they were to go public. Nevertheless, the matter had been discussed by the board. It would make Besier's job easier if SAP was listed on the New York Stock Exchange, as it would improve investors' awareness of SAP. His position was that without disclosure according to United States standards, investors would not understand the whole extent of SAP's activities, whereas they could easily inform themselves about Microsoft and Sybase at any time. But by saying this, Besier was openly criticizing SAP's course.

Besier's Departure

At the beginning of January 1996, Paul Wahl learned that he was to be Klaus Besier's successor at the top of SAP America. Wahl—who had managed the launch of R/3 in the United States from his post in Walldorf and was a member of the extended management board—was not surprised. Besier had made a visit to Walldorf for a meeting with CEO Dietmar Hopp, and when Wahl joined the meeting, Hopp told him: "Mr. Besier has decided to leave SAP."

Three weeks later, on January 31, 1996, the change was announced in a short press release: "Klaus Besier, president and CEO of SAP America, Inc., leaves SAP today. He will join Business@Web, a United States software provider, based in Cambridge, Massachusetts, as CEO and chairman of the worldwide business. Paul Wahl, age forty-three, has been appointed Besier's successor." A year and a half later, when Besier was asked what his biggest mistake had been in his time with SAP, he answered: "Jumping from one firm to the next without taking time for the right decision."

Hasso Plattner explained Besier's sudden departure this way: "When Klaus Besier took over as head of SAP America four years ago, our objective was to increase the sales revenue for 1995 to $500 million. At $710 million, we significantly exceeded this ambitious goal. Of course, we regret Klaus Besier's decision." But Wahl's succession as well as the new release, 3.0, of R/3 "will guarantee that SAP will maintain its dominant market position and will continue to be successful in this market," explained a short bulletin issued by the company.

But with Besier's exit, analysts wondered about SAP's direction. Only a few weeks after Besier left, Forrester Research, in Cambridge, Massachusetts, prepared a report that was pessimistic about what the shift in leadership meant for the German company in a world in which the Internet was expected to play an increasingly important role. This analysis made headlines in Germany, too, and promptly triggered a sharp tumble in SAP's share price from its September 1995 high of $181.80 to $126.67 in May 1996. If, as the analysts wrote, SAP introduced its next-generation product (dubbed "R/10" by Forrester), R/3 would soon be branded an "unattractive, previous-generation product." Or, as German business daily *Handelsblatt* put it: "A museum piece."

There was no R/10, or R/4, the more likely version number which was adopted by the press when reporting Forrester's findings—findings that had to be revisited shortly thereafter. SAP, having grown to the size of a global giant, might have slowed down in the process. But the behemoth, it found out soon, had heard the Internet wake-up call.

Chapter Six

Systems Implementation— "Being Sold Down the River"

There is a big demand for consulting services. However, management consulting is anything but transparent, and most inscrutable is the market for IT consulting.

—Jörg Staute

What do you get by implementing R/3? IT managers, consultants, developers, and competitors of SAP agree: It's all in the company's name.

Although the acronym is as meaningless as any in the software industry, it made for a fitting analogy when the high costs of SAP implementations became an issue in the business press: "All this, of course, is going to make you feel that SAP's name is all too appropriate," wrote *Fortune*, "as the money flows out of your company like maple sap in the springtime."

But there is much more to this name, according to Christian Schaefer from the University of Dortmund, Germany. Asking around in the SAP community, the R/3 specialist has compiled a telling Web list of unofficial SAP definitions (http://www.ruhr.de/home/calle2/sap.html), featuring interpretations in German, English, and French, as well as in Bavarian.

If nothing else, the list accurately reflects the mixed reception

SAP still gets in the corporate world—the commercial success of R/3 notwithstanding. Schaefer's definitions range from "Super Application Programs" to "Such a Pain." They tell of "Shock, Angst and Panic (on the user level)," advise employees to "Submit and Pray," and recommend to "Send Another Payment," or even to "Select Another Package." As for the company and its shareholders, Schaefer found, SAP still spells "Siphon Away Profits."

Christopher Everett, head of SAP consulting services at Price Waterhouse, recalled in *Fortune* magazine: "We'd never heard of SAP before, but we sent three guys to Germany to talk to them. They came back looking like Charlton Heston as Moses, all white as he came down from the mountain. They had seen the vision of what this could be." Price Waterhouse's enthusiasm increased when, five years later, SAP launched R/3, the first integrated standard applications software for client-server computing.

The reason for their enthusiasm? First, companies flocked to purchase R/3 because it made their operations leaner and more efficient, allowing them to serve their customers better. Second, R/3 provided a bonanza for consultants; according to conservative estimates, for each dollar that is spent on SAP software, users must spend another two to four dollars for service and consulting in implementing the system. In Germany alone, companies spent $840 million for SAP-related services in 1995. Therefore, large auditing and consulting companies such as Arthur Andersen, Coopers & Lybrand, Ernst & Young, ICS/Deloitte & Touche, KPMG, and Price Waterhouse benefit from SAP's growth. Leading computer manufacturers such as DEC, Hewlett-Packard, IBM, and Siemens Nixdorf are among the consulting partners of SAP, too, as are more than a hundred smaller computer manufacturers. As of December 1997 SAP directly employed some 4,200 software professionals in the consulting business, and there were another 30,000 external SAP consultants worldwide.

For many SAP customers, implementing the sophisticated standard enterprise software calls for sometimes radical reorganization of business processes that can be managed only with support from external consultants. Of course, it is true that software from SAP's competitors, such as Baan, J. D. Edwards, Oracle, and PeopleSoft, cannot be implemented without support from external consultants, either. This fact is often ignored by SAP's critics. But there is a difference between SAP and its competitors insofar as support from external consultants is concerned: SAP became the leading provider of enterprise software by integrating this squadron of external consultants into its sales strategy.

SAP chose to pursue this strategy for two reasons. First, by doing so it avoided the overspending that would result from assigning its own staff to implement the sophisticated standard software. Second, by doing it this way, SAP managed to avoid competing with the large consulting firms and computer manufacturers who were its partners. "We will not compete with our partners," stated SAP manager Alexander Ott, who was in charge of strategic alliances. "We don't believe we're big project management guys." Added Ott: "We believe we have the best product knowledge."

Right from the start, consulting firms were involved in the mega-business of SAP R/3. United States analysts applauded the German company's choice of strategy. Hasso Plattner remembers: "We could as well have become a consulting firm for sophisticated business administration." And he adds dryly: "We could as well have become a firm without any focus."

The partner strategy of SAP was praised as a "brilliant move" by many in the media, too. For example, in January 1995 the German newspaper *Frankfurter Allgemeine Zeitung* quoted Peter Thilo Huber, an analyst from Bayerische Vereinsbank, who enthusiastically praised SAP's strategy; he spoke of consulting companies that "recommend" SAP software to their clients. Yet barely two months later, the magazine *Wirtschaftswoche* published a controversial cover story on SAP in which it used the term "selling" to describe what SAP's logo partners did. Apparently the word was what SAP objected to, and it spent several hundred thousand dollars on an advertising campaign to counteract that impression. In one of the ads, for example, Klaus Ploenzke,

CEO of CSC Ploenzke AG, explained: "We protest the implication that we sell software on behalf of SAP."

Did Bayerische Vereinsbank and *Frankfurter Allgemeine Zeitung* misunderstand the relation among SAP, consultants, and customers? Hardly. Consultants often serve as software providers, "door openers" to the executive floor. They also are likely to have a say in the reorganization of data processing in any company they work for. Afterward, application consultants help to implement the new software. The muddle about the role of external consultants is explained by, among other things, conflicting impressions of the consulting industry—particularly among midsized enterprises.

Companies had not yet forgotten the inglorious performance of IT consultants in the 1970s and 1980s, when consultants talked smaller firms into buying powerful mainframe computers by IBM or other manufacturers but just a few years later recommended to those same clients that they outsource data processing. Jörg Staute, an expert on the software industry, warns in his book *The Consulting Report:* "Consultants are technology enthusiasts. They convey the faith in endless possibilities for improvement through technology. They believe that each organizational problem can be solved with the appropriate data processing equipment and optimal IT system."

Staute calls IT consulting a "gray area between consulting and selling." In contrast to other types of consulting, it is always a question of buying hardware and software. Staute takes this view: "Today, each company is dependent on external support in the field of IT. Consultants act as gatekeepers who determine how the money is spent." Therefore, they often orient themselves by the market leader—in the past IBM, currently SAP. Some take a less neutral view; in 1994 Dieter Eckbauer, then editor in chief of *Computerwoche*, said, " 'Independent' consultants—don't make me laugh!"

"Software vendors are attempting to capitalize on our relationships and our positions with our respective clients," explains Herb Vinnicombe, a Coopers & Lybrand partner in Philadelphia. However, he adds: "None of us can afford to associate with a product that can't stand up to scrutiny." After all, the reputation of the relevant consulting firm is at stake. The consultants are obliged to their clients, not to the software vendors, as Vinnicombe points out: "We're not selling on behalf of them."

For the consultants, the actual business starts after the client buys SAP software. As most consultants charge by the hour, the longer the software implementation takes, the better for the consultant. But in order to penetrate the market segment of midsized companies, SAP had to reduce its implementation costs, both by changing the software to make the process simpler and by taking the consultants in hand. Otherwise, there was a danger that what was to the consultants' benefit could become SAP's disadvantage. The market research firm Input stated that SAP was confronted with "the challenge of managing a maturing business which clearly requires a different strategic and operational approach to that involved in pure entrepreneurial management."

"IT consultant" is not a protected job title. In the enterprise software business, the boundaries between consulting, system consulting, and applications consulting blur. Undoubtedly, there are consultants with dubious references. Because of this, and because of the possibility of the appearance of a conflict of interest, SAP's high dependency on consulting firms might, in 1994, have promoted a dangerous rumor that promptly lowered the share price of SAP: the rumor that SAP had been infiltrated by members of the Church of Scientology, which had been branded by German officials as a "criminal" cult. Regardless, the SAP founders made the decision to tie their company—come what may—to consulting firms. In turn, their consulting partners considerably contributed to the success of standard software by contributing business know-how or by developing innovative add-on programs and customized R/2 and R/3 applications for specific sectors of industry.

So, for example, Hans-Georg Plaut is regarded as one of the godfathers of SAP software. Plaut, who died in 1992, developed a Methodology of Activity Based Cost and Profit Contribution Margin Management, founded a consulting firm, and specialized in business software for large and midsized enterprises. Hasso Plattner recalls that a visit to Plaut he made with Dietmar Hopp decisively influenced the development of SAP.

"We closed a deal," explains Plattner. "We took over his heritage in business administration, developed the software on the basis of that, and built it into R/2 and integrated it into R/3 later." Before this, SAP was "more technically oriented," says Plattner. "Our focus had been real-time processing and integration of application programs. Our work was more about technology than business administration." But Plattner describes the cooperation with Plaut as a turning point for SAP." For example, the concepts of R/2 module RK and R/3 module CO go back to Plaut.

The first strategic partner among the Big Six that SAP that managed to win was Price Waterhouse in 1989. Price Waterhouse developed templates of industry-specific business processes by which the implementation of R/3 could be standardized for specific sectors of industry. In 1995 Price Waterhouse established in Philadelphia the first global training center for SAP experts. As another example, SAP used the expertise of Andersen Consulting in the oil and gas industry to help it enter this market segment.

However, at times SAP had to pay a high price for such profitable cooperation with consulting firms. Whenever one of their consultant partners was the subject of negative media attention, SAP and its software were in the pillory, too. And anytime a consultant was responsible for something like a badly planned R/3 implementation, it reflected poorly on SAP as well. "There is almost no other opportunity by which you can waste so much money as state-of-the-art technology that cements senseless business processes," warns Jörg Staute.

Top consulting firms contributed to the unprecedented success of R/3 in the United States by opening the door to the executive floor. But the gold-digger attitude of consulting firms concerning R/3 and the scarcity of qualified SAP experts—particularly in the United States—led to a situation in which SAP increasingly was assessed by the quality of its consultants. In 1996 the market research firm Input warned that the situation in the consulting market would come to a head in the late 1990s.

Critics complained that SAP long ago lost control of external consultants. Those same consultants, however, take quite a different view: "SAP can dictate whatever it wants," says Jay Rosenfeld, from the consulting firm BSG. SAP is such a powerhouse that it can get its contractual terms—for example, rules governing liability—accepted by consulting firms that wish to do business with it.

With a sophisticated two-tier concept for involving strategic alliance partners, SAP tries to organize the market and to lower the costs for implementation of R/3 through controlled competitive pressure. In the top tier are logo partners, which are classified as either global, national, or regional strategic partners. They enjoy privileges at SAP. For example, in 1994 SAP had forty-four logo partners in Germany. In the second tier are implementation partners. Mostly these are smaller consulting firms. In particular, SAP entrusted the selling of R/3 and consulting about its implementation in midsized enterprises to what are called "R/3 system houses."

"Through the two-tier partner concept SAP stopped the uncontrolled growth of unauthorized service providers for implementation of R/3," attests analyst Frank Jestczemski, of Input. But this did not lead to increased transparency in the market.

Do clients and users of SAP software really benefit from these strategic alliances? Can they really rely on their expensive external consultants to independently support them to the best of their knowledge in optimizing their business and information processes?

Case Study of a Successful Implementation

The University Clinic Rudolf Virchow in Berlin-Wedding, Germany, which had merged with the famous Charité University Clinic in Berlin, had to be reorganized. Up to sixty thousand patients pass through its doors each year. But the clinic did not have an effective system for patient management. In up to a fifth of cases, records could not be found and had to be reconstructed—sometimes more than once.

The administration was reorganized in record time. With an investment of $11.3 million, fifteen hospitals in Berlin implemented a new computer system in order to improve efficiency and cost-effectiveness. This system was based on R/3 Healthcare, a concept that had been designed for the integration of all areas of a hospital: administration, nursing, and medical treatment.

The R/3 module IS-H (industry-specific health care) handles

- Management of inpatients and outpatients
- Settlement of patient accounts
- Controlling day-to-day hospital operations
- Internal and external data exchange (e.g., with other hospitals)

This system makes it possible for all patient data to be retrieved for patients who already have records there. Duplicate treatments can be avoided. And experts estimate that 50 percent of physician's reports could be eliminated by means of the integrated system for diagnosis coding.

Redundancies and transmission errors were eliminated, too. The computer investigates the costs of any given treatment, and the data can be accessed by the accounts department. "Hospitals achieved cost reductions of several million dollars," explained SAP expert Lutz Völker.

In 1996 more than 120 hospitals already used SAP software. The SAP implementation in Berlin set an example not only because of its size, but also for the speed with which the system was implemented. Five hospitals implemented the system within four months because they were well advised by Siemens Nixdorf, which had been the main contractor for the implementation of R/3 in over seventy hospitals. This software solution is to a large extent made possible by the know-how of SAP experts from Siemens Nixdorf. As a global partner of SAP, Siemens Nixdorf serves some one thousand R/3 installations worldwide. For the implementation in the Berlin hospitals, Siemens Nixdorf experts used a software system called R/3 Live. Originally this toolkit had been developed to accelerate R/3 implementation in midsized enterprises. But it was found to work well with large sites, too.

Evaluation of Service Providers

In 1996 the market research firm Input in Langgöns, Germany, asked 450 users of SAP R/3 to evaluate leading SAP service providers. The top four were, in order, Siemens Nixdorf, CSC Ploenzke AG, Debis Systemhaus, and SAP AG. The Big Six had been ranked only as mediocre because SAP users often criticized the disproportion between costs and benefits.

On the other side of the Atlantic, *Datamation* summarized a study on the performance of SAP service providers that had been done by the market research firm Gartner Group and which had somewhat different results. Three of the Bix Six firms—Andersen, ICS/Deloitte & Touche, and Price Waterhouse—were ranked as strong everywhere. Two other Big Six firms—Ernst & Young and KPMG—were ranked as strong in Europe and average elsewhere. Siemens Nixdorf was ranked as average in Europe and strong elsewhere.

Empirical Study on R/3 Implementation

Implementations such as that in the Berlin hospitals are the type of success story of which SAP consultants boast. But that is not the rule. As we've seen, the implementation of standard enterprise software can drag on for several years.

The first empirical study on R/3 implementation in Europe was presented in the spring of 1996 by Gemini Consulting in cooperation with the University of Frankfurt. Two hundred twenty SAP implementations in large and midsized enterprises were analyzed.

The companies studied implemented between three and nine R/3 modules (release 2.1 or 2.2). On average, the time required for implementation was fifteen months and the project budget was $2 million.

The conclusion of Peter Buxmann from the Institute of Business Information Science at the University of Frankfurt, was: "If companies increasingly use standard enterprise software, competitive advantages can be gained only through a more effective implementation."

How quickly R/3 can be put into place may be as crucial for a company as the selection of appropriate software modules and a powerful hardware platform. But in the fall of 1996 Peter Zencke, a member of the SAP board, frankly admitted: "Sometimes there are conflicting interests. In any case, the intention of SAP is to implement R/3 quickly, whereas consulting firms may be tempted to get a job for as many employees as possible." But the Gemini study showed that consulting firms cannot be blamed in all cases where the implementation period was unduly long.

One problem, surprisingly enough, was management at the companies implementing R/3. Sixty-three percent of the SAP R/3 implementations that were analyzed by Gemini had been initiated by management itself. Nevertheless, executives showed surprisingly little interest in the implementation phase of the project. "Obviously, the decision makers didn't recognize the need to make decisions," explained Buxmann.

In cases where this happens, the real source of the implementation problems may not be recognized. Often, the software or the consultants are blamed. Vinnie Mirchandani, a software expert from the Gartner Group, warns that companies choose integrators "based on handshakes, résumés, and two-page RFPs, and then come back and blame the integrators. Some fault lies with the companies themselves for not running a better process."

It's clear that the selection of consultants often determines whether the R/3 implementation will become a success story or a nightmare. It can be difficult to distinguish true experts from high-tech crooks in the rapidly growing market for SAP services. Some software providers deceive their clients with wrong data about SAP project experience or the technical competence of their consultants. Mirchandani sums it up this way: "The SAP software itself is okay, but the service quality of consulting firms is very sketchy."

Some SAP implementations turn out to be an absolute disaster, as was the case with a failed R/2 implementation at a United States chemical company with a project budget of $200 million. Others lead to a user rebellion. During the implementation of SAP software at the publishing company Bantam Doubleday Dell, memos regarding the implementation read as follows: "Lost many orders due to their warehouse switch," "New computer system total chaos and disaster," and so on. Sometimes bizarre episodes occur. For a daily rate of $1,000, a company in Munich hired a consultant to standardize the documentation. Says a company insider, "But when we fired him after a fortnight, the bulging file contained almost exclusively empty pages with perfectly formatted footers."

How to Select Consultants for Systems Implementation

Which Consulting Firms Are Worth the Money?

"Software is too important to be left to IT professionals"—this recommendation was made by none other than SAP cofounder Klaus Tschira. Not even the illustrious name of a high-priced consulting firm guarantees the success of the planned R/3 implementation.

In order to avoid a flop costing several million dollars, the customer should carefully check the references of the prospective team leader and team members. Comprehensive industry and software knowledge is important, too.

- The team leader should have successfully completed at least one comparable R/3 implementation. Sufficient team members with SAP experience should be assigned as well. Often the scarcity of SAP consultants leads to a situation in which most team members are relative novices.
- The assigned consultants should have sound and versatile

knowledge in the industry sector of the client. Otherwise, the customer risks being a guinea pig for newly certified SAP junior consultants.

- The name of the assigned team leader should be included in the contract, and it should be agreed that any changes in important team personnel must be approved by the customer. Due to fierce competition for lucrative orders for R/3 implementation, it has become a common practice in the software industry to promise the same star consultant to several prospective customers at the same time.

- The selected service provider should take into account the experience of other customers (e.g., in the same industry), so that costs and length of implementation can be reduced by sharing experts or by using well-tried software tools for the configuration of the system.

- The consultants should know all about the kinks and quirks of R/3. Only experts who know the weak points are able to assess whether software for functions that are not covered by R/3 should be developed or purchased from a third-party software provider.

- The prospective consultants should be compatible with the customer's corporate culture, because they do not come and go overnight but will work in the company for several months.

- The business objectives should be kept in sight at all times. The new software, after all, is only a means to an end. When the software is finally implemented, for example, the throughput time (i.e., order processing, production time, and delivery time) should be reduced substantially compared to benchmarking results.

Reasons for typical difficulties in implementing SAP R/3 are:

- **The high degree of integration of R/3** The complex interrelationship between the different SAP modules is one of the most important advantages of the system. But it is precisely this integration that makes the implementation more difficult. For example, in R/3 a purchase order can be defined as a "standard order," "instructions for delivery," or a "basic contract." Thousands of software switches must be defined free of error—this requires a full understanding of the relevant business processes. For example, parameters that are defined in the module for Sales and Distribution (SD) influence other modules of the system, for instance, the module for controlling (CO).

- **Special requests of customers for sophisticated add-on functions** The more the standard software will be modified, the trickier the implementation will be. Martin Boll, a consultant at SAP in Walldorf, explains, "In plain language: I can achieve 80 percent of the objectives with 20 percent of my effort. But for the residual 20 percent I must use 80 percent of my effort. This is, after all, a question of cost for the customer."

- **Vague objectives and a poor implementation strategy** "You have to treat SAP as a business, rather than an IT, project," emphasizes Karl Newkirk, of Andersen Consulting. "Success comes from having a very clear idea of how you want to run the business and then using R/3 to enforce the way you've modeled it."

- **Insufficient coordination** Integrated standard software largely abolishes the existing departmental organization structure. It depends on the management whether employees will understood this as an opportunity or as a threat. Simply involving employee committees or unions in systems implementation is not enough. "The employees in the operating departments groan when they learn responsibility will be assigned to them"—this is the experience of organization consultant Bruno Grupp. On the other hand, the process model of SAP R/3, which is thought out down to the last detail, can lead someone to prescribe R/3 in a top-down approach. That is "a bad mistake," warns Karl Schmitz, from TSE in Hamburg, who supported more than a hundred companies in SAP implementations.

- **Scarcity of qualified SAP experts** "Rarely before has the computer marketplace created a demand that so dramatically outstrips supply," wrote *Computer World*. The implementation teams, recruited in a hurry, often consist of inexperienced IROCs—"idiots right out of college," mocked managers in the United States.

However, Bruce Richardson, from the market research firm Advanced Manufacturing Research in Boston, Massachusetts, emphasizes that "there's a lot of pain involved" when it comes to large ERP software installations, and "it's not exclusive to SAP." But increased competition, growing cost pressures, and the globalization of markets—e-commerce on the Internet, too—forced many enterprises to go through this process and to redefine their structure and business processes.

Such a redefinition, in which all obsolete information systems will be supplemented or fully replaced, requires organizational, business, and strategic concepts for which external consultants usually must be called in. Nevertheless, midsized companies increasingly put up with the troubles of converting their data processing to client-server standard software from SAP. The highly integrated standard software by which data processing can be standardized step by step or in one go was regarded as the key for the management challenge of the 1990s: business process reengineering (BPR).

Business Process Reengineering

This term was coined by United States management consultants Michael Hammer and James Champy. In their book *Reengineering the Corporation: A Manifesto for Business Revolution*, they defined *reengineering* as "fundamental rethinking and radical redesign of business processes to achieve dramatic improvements in critical, contemporary measures of performance, such as cost, quality, service, and speed." Because of the divisions of process that were a legacy of Taylorism, the vision of the total business process got lost. Michael Hammer holds the view that IT must be used in a creative way in order to achieve a "radical change." Until recently, IT had been used only to mechanize traditional business processes. But Michael Hammer, a computer scientist who lectures at MIT, made the following points:

- Information processing should be subsumed into the real work that produces the information.
- Geographically dispersed resources should be treated as if they were centralized.
- The "decision point" should be put where the work is performed.
- Information should be captured only once—"at the source."

Economists in the United States found that investments in IT initiated more than half of all reengineering projects. However, 70 percent of all reengineering projects ended with poor results, admitted Hammer in 1995. One of the main dangers is that companies can waste their energy on a poorly planned change, making them unable to keep up with competitors' new products or services. One prominent example was American Express, which subjected its credit card business to a comprehensive reengineering effort. While they were engaged in this, MasterCard and Visa launched a new product—the corporate procurement card. It took a full year before American Express could offer the same service to its customers.

But the experience of American Express need not be universal. "Today, IT is much more than a tool for optimizing the workflow; it is an engine for business process redesign," says Gerhard Keller, expert for R/3 process methods at SAP. "The big reengineering peak is not behind us, but ahead of us," forecasts Bruno Rücker, a member of the board of CSC Ploenzke AG. However, the emerging trend, in contrast to what happened in the first half of the 1990s, is to place greater importance on the "human dimension." James Moffatt, of Coopers & Lybrand in Philadelphia, points out that "you need the buy-in of all the employees in order to make the changes in people's jobs that the software will impose." Cross-sectional cooperation and joint training often lead to a change of mind-set for the employees—and that can be a critical factor in the success of the implementation.

SAP under Pressure

For all of the reasons discussed earlier, SAP increasingly came under pressure in the mid-1990s. "We have invested much in order to reduce the manpower requirements for implementing our software," said Dietmar Hopp at the end of 1994. But a few months later he responded angrily to criticism in the magazines *Computerwoche* and *Wirtschaftswoche* that the rigidity of SAP R/3 drove users to depend too much on external consultants. "The same critics that complain about R/3's inflexibility also complain about its high complexity," explained Hopp in *Wirtschaftswoche*. "You must decide: Will you have a simple PC software that cannot be adjusted, or a software such as SAP R/3 that is adjustable and, therefore, is necessarily complex? Both together is not possible."

Though Hopp was on the defensive in his public comments, internally SAP was already working at full speed toward technical and organizational solutions in order to simplify the implementation of R/3. In August 1995, in an interview with the business news service VWD, Hopp acknowledged the problems and announced that SAP had established a worldwide operating task force to track down potential implementation trouble spots and offer support. Hopp's reasoning was this: "You can sell software most easily if you have many examples of cost-effective implementation."

For that purpose SAP had developed a powerful software tool intended to simplify and accelerate the implementation of R/3: the "Business Engineering Workbench." A German consulting firm, a spin-off of the University of Saarbrücken, contributed to this development.

BPR Tools—Software for Modeling Work Flows

At a lecture in October 1992 Professor August-Wilhelm Scheer presented to an audience of consultants, software experts, and technical journalists his concept of the "paperless consultant."

At that time, almost no consultant visited a customer with a laptop or notebook computer, and the "paperless office," once a dream of Heinz Nixdorf, was still regarded as a long-term technological objective. Was the notion of a "paperless consultant," therefore, the quirk of a naive scholar? Industry experts knew better. The author of the German standard textbook *Data Processing–Oriented Business Administration—Basis of Information Management* (1984) and other books had received numerous awards and not only was regarded as a grandmaster of theory in his field but had already shown a great affinity for practice—quite unusual for a German professor. For years his university department closely cooperated with SAP; looking back, Scheer said: "SAP was not yet on the front pages then." Scheer, director of the Institute of Business Informatics, was also the founder and main partner of IDS Scheer (Company for Integrated Data Processing Systems Ltd.). He himself joined SAP's board of directors in 1988.

As Scheer developed it, the concept of a "paperless consultant" involved multipurpose software tools by means of which the implementation of enterprise software could be automated. "Our intention is to start this project on a large scale," announced Scheer.

The ARIS toolset of IDS is a collection of simple-to-handle software tools. The acronym ARIS stands for "architecture of integrated information systems." ARIS is designed to simplify the configuration of standard enterprise software such as SAP R/3, and it helped SAP to accelerate the implementation of R/3. Through ARIS, IDS became the market leader for BPR tools. By the spring of 1997, Scheer had sold seven thousand licenses, and his company had six hundred employees. It had developed into a worldwide company with subsidiaries in the United States and Switzerland as well as joint ventures in South America, South Korea, and South Africa.

Parts of ARIS were included in SAP's Business Engineering Workbench, which was launched in May 1996. "By means of ARIS, users can define and simulate complete business processes on the basis of R/3 process models—from optimization of work flows to configuration of R/3 to documentation to training of users," explains Stefan Meinhardt, an expert on implementation methods and tools at SAP. ARIS is linked to the R/3 Business Repository—a built-in description of some eight hundred business processes. The business repository, for example, contains a description of the process of placing purchase orders—including the selection of material and a supplier as well as following up on orders already placed. Another example is order processing, which covers pricing, terms and conditions, collecting, and route planning for shipment. Commented Scheer: "R/3 is leading in the field of business process modeling."

What Scheer noticed is that in describing work flow, there is often language confusion between the employees who are affected by a reorganization. So the clerk in purchase order processing, the controller, the IT professional, and/or the external consultant (using SAP-speak) often use quite different terms for the same facts. Scheer's ideas was that in order to overcome this difficulty, standard enterprise software must provide a sort of digital assistant that would pave the way on-site at the customer's office for the integration of information processing.

Meanwhile, state-of-the-art modeling software serves as a translator between operating departments, business administration, and data processing. But this software offers still more. With the SAP reference model (R/3 Business Repository), complex company models can be simulated on the PC screen, fine-tuned, and afterward transmitted to the newly installed R/3 system as an order for configuration. For that purpose, what are called event-controlled process chains are presented. Such flow charts describe the relevant operation through standardized symbols and standard terms from business administration.

The interactive symbols are programmed in such a way that they work like switches in an intelligent railroad system, allowing for a multitude of alternative junctions and automatically warning against line obstacles or dead ends. So, for example, if the start event "demand arises" occurs, the reason might be that an employee in production needs material from the warehouse. The system leads to the stage "allocation of purchase order," in which the criteria for the purchase order are defined. Scheer explained that the implementation of standard enterprise software "is not only a technical problem. In many cases it will take the longest time to find out which solution a company really needs."

In this phase, the most important tool for the consultant is an analysis program that can be used to describe the work flow of the customer. Through a target-performance comparison, the weak points of business functions and data exchange can be detected. For this analysis the IDS program Analyzer is used; it does not yet need a link to R/3.

When the route is defined, the modeling system can be linked with R/3 in order to set the course on the basis of the model's assumptions. However, the models must have been developed on the basis of the R/3 Business Repository. Thus, the notorious parameterization of several thousand R/3 switch tables can be automated to a large extent. An additional special-purpose program helps in fine-tuning the digital switches: the implementation guide (IMG). The IMG guides the user through the implementation process. SAP expert Stefan Meinhardt emphasized the future importance of such tools: "Users want to implement their standard enterprise software as quickly as possible. Afterward they will look for continuous process improvements."

According to the same principle SAP designed its Business Engineering Workbench—now renamed the Business Engineer—which can be linked to the ARIS toolset. Peter Zencke explains: "Because business and the general economic setting change faster than long-term projects can, in the course of a reengineering discussion management should determine the top corporate objectives and define those core processes from whose acceleration the company can benefit."

In the meantime, competitors to ARIS entered the market, including LiveModel for R/3, from IntelliCorp, and Business Modeler, from Visio. SAP saw to it that these programs can all be used in combination with the Business Engineer from SAP. In fact, since the spring of 1997, SAP has favored LiveModel; SAP took an equity stake of 14 percent in IntelliCorp in 1996. So the connection to IDS "no longer has the exclusive character it did in the past," explains Zencke.

However, the openness of SAP is no issue, says Zencke. "The ARIS toolset is open, too. It supports—in addition to what is needed for SAP R/3—other modeling methods, too." Professor Scheer also emphasizes that IDS tries "to follow a strategy that is independent of SAP." In 1996 the proportion of IDS's sales that were related to SAP consulting was still some 60 percent; in the product area, the proportion of SAP-related development was about 30 percent. ARIS is also used for implementing competitive software (e.g., products from Baan). IDS customers include Daimler-Benz, Volkswagen, Deutsche Telekom, Akzo Nobel, and Samsung.

The success of R/3 was reflected in the financial statements of IDS, too. IDS achieved growth rates similar to SAP's. In 1996 the sales revenue of IDS increased by 47 percent, to $58.7 million; its foreign business doubled, to 43 percent, and the labor force increased by 36 percent, to 536 employees. IDS went public in May 1999, following the example of SAP (which holds an 18.14 percent stake in the company), and offered a profit-sharing scheme to its employees. Says Scheer, "Companies such as us depend on the motivation of their employees. We have to be good and quick." IDS opened branches in Japan and Singapore as well.

Another thing Scheer has asked for is more transparency in the systems integrators. His novel software tools should contribute to such transparency in the consulting business as well as cost reduction.

His concept is reflected in SAP's software. "With our Business Engineering Workbench we can document what external consultants did at the customer's office—and we can make it transparent to the user, explained Peter Zencke in 1996. It documents all selling activities, process selections, and customizing activities in such a way that the customer obtains a knowledge database that can be used in the future. "Therefore, the customer is not dependent on the consultant who did the first implementation," concluded Zencke.

The Consultants Crisis—
Turnover of SAP Professionals

Kevin Funk was with the *Seattle Times*, the largest daily newspaper in the Northwest, for an unusually long time—thirteen years. Then came SAP. And Kevin Funk was gone.

Funk familiarized himself with SAP R/3 when the *Seattle Times* implemented R/3 in 1993, as one of the first customers in the United States. Soon the newly minted R/3 expert trained his colleagues in how to use the multipurpose software. The new knowledge paid off for Funk when he was lured away, with a 35 percent raise, by the consulting firm ICS/Deloitte & Touche. Many consultants can tell a similar story.

The camera manufacturer Pentax, in Englewood, Colorado, for example, lost within one year four of its twelve R/3 implementation experts. Anyone who decides on SAP, warns Randy Lewis, director of information services at Lyondell Petrochemical in Houston, Texas, should safeguard the loyalty of his experts. Otherwise, says this manager, "you'll watch $20,000 in training and $100,000 worth of experience walk out the door." And the trade magazine *Datamation* warned its readers—mostly IT managers of large and midsized companies—"Chain your staff down."

Even with top salaries, SAP customers could not hold their R/3 professionals, because as SAP consultants they can earn dream fees. Consultants who previously had a yearly income of $50,000 to $60,000 can earn $85,000 to $90,000 after one year of R/3 experience. The exodus of R/3-trained IT professionals from companies that implemented R/3 actually put the reputation of SAP in the United States at risk—not just because company employees left, but because their replacements, sent in by external firms, charged astronomical fees and often had minimal experience. Plus they "never get the same consultant twice. You never know what's in store for you at the next upgrade," complained an IT manager.

In Germany the consultants crisis reached its first peak in March 1995 with the controversial cover story in *Wirtschaftswoche* revealing that the daily rate of an external IT professional was $1,400; in case of emergency the daily rate might even be as high as $5,600. Dietmar Hopp furiously countered this story in a large-scale media campaign, saying, "Fifty-six hundred dollars is totally unfounded. I would call it blackmail." Even at a more modest level, the Big Six still charged up to $500 per hour, reported analysts from the Gartner Group and Forrester Research in 1996. Furthermore, market research firms and consulting firms reported dubious data and engaged in statistical juggling tricks in order to distinguish themselves in the lucrative SAP market. So SAP's competitors could rub their hands in glee when United States analysts reported that the ratio between software and service costs was 1:7 to 1:10—and simply neglect to mention that these figures could include reengineering expenditures not related to SAP.

It is true that the implementation of R/3 could be simplified considerably by means of improved software tools such as the Business Engineering Workbench. "We must get to a stage where R/3 users can implement R/3 with normal employees—not only with people who have Ph.D.s," commented Hasso Plattner at the SAP user conference in August 1996. While SAP could not yet control the job market for R/3 consultants, it responded with increased quality measures and an expansion of its training program. In 1996, for example, they introduced performance controls for consulting firms. "Now we can find out whether an implementation is quick or slow," explains Peter Zencke. "Our own professionals define model cases and prove that it is possible to carry out lean implementations quickly and with high quality."

Training Programs

According to an analysis of the job market by DEKRA Academy in Stuttgart, Germany, in 1996 SAP experts had been the most sought-after IT professionals in Germany, and analysts from Input even expected the situation to get worse. The reasons were the increasing number of SAP users migrating from R/2 to R/3 and the brain drain of experienced consultants to the United States. Market analysts estimated a demand for more than nine thousand R/3 consultants in Germany up to 1998. In order to meet the increasing demand better, SAP intensified its training measures. In Germany, 50 percent of the consultants were trained by SAP itself. The others attended training programs run by SAP partners.

In the spring of 1997, the DEKRA Academy entered into a contract with SAP allowing standardized SAP training materials to be used in R/3 education programs supported by public institutions. In agreeing to this, SAP was trying to better control the qualifications of IT professionals. Every year three thousand new consultants are trained worldwide. At the beginning of 1997 SAP admitted that "we cannot meet the actual demand of the market and establish better transparency due to the often inevitably short vocational experience of the consultants. Therefore, professional and effective certification of SAP know-how is absolutely necessary."

In the computer industry, certificates are regarded as an effective measure to tie partner firms and training organizers to the products of a company. Novell was the first large IT company to use this approach, and now it awards the title Certified Novell Engineer (CNE) to IT professionals who go through comprehensive training and pass specialized tests. At Microsoft, according to information given by the firm, a total of more than eighty thousand IT professionals have completed the Microsoft Certified Professional Program. Often IT professionals are forced to pay for such certificates, as the market power of the supplier and the quality requests of its customers will accept no less. The graduate of a similar program in Walldorf is called an "SAP Certified R/3 Consultant" (as opposed to just "SAP consultant," which has no official status at SAP). In the course, their knowledge of the programming language ABAP/4 is tested by computer. For example, for the subject "batch input" the examinee is asked on the PC screen: "What are the contents of the fields SY-SUBRC, CONT, FLAG after execution of the IMPORT instruction? Please click on the button next to the right answer." The multimedia tests were developed by the smallest subsidiary of SAP: AsseT GmbH in Friedrichshafen, Germany. The purpose of this company is "to make consulting competence a measurable variable."

"This is not a guarantee that a person knows what he's talking about or can now charge $1,500 a day," admits Alexander Ott, SAP manager for strategic alliances. However, it is "one more benchmark to know who has substance and who doesn't. The objective is that in the long run only certified consultants should implement R/3."

Calibrated Test of Consultants

Through computerized certification of consultants, SAP tries to improve the quality of the customer support for R/3. The programs have been developed by clever software tinkerers from Friedrichshafen, Germany.

When Michael Habon, the founder of AsseT, looks out of his office window in Friedrichshafen at Lake Constance, he sees neither white sails nor the Swiss Alps. Instead the entrepreneur looks at the parking lot of Debis, the IT branch of Daimler-Benz AG. A young company, AsseT leases space in Debis's building.

The smallest subsidiary of SAP, in its first fiscal year AsseT had sales of $1.7 million. Its customers include Mannesmann Mobilfunk, VEAG, Danzas, EDS, and Siemens.

The firm (Internet: www.assett-online.com) specializes in developing multimedia test and training software. It plays a key role in SAP's intention to make the worldwide market for R/3 services more transparent through calibrated tests for consultants. The AsseT software Advanced Certification Environment (ACE) guarantees that tests conform to the latest release of R/3 as well as provide standardized grades.

By means of ACE, eighty multiple-choice tasks are presented to the examinee on the PC screen in the test center over a period of three hours. R/3 knowledge, analytical talent, and judgment are all examined. In 1996 sixteen hundred consultants were tested with ACE. SAP plans to replace the paper-and-pencil tests that are practiced in the United States with ACE.

The first product developed by Habon and his team of nine psychologists and IT professionals was Assessment Excellence (AE)—special-purpose software for personnel consultants that helps in preparing job specifications and allows the assessment of candidates by core competencies such as ability to learn, organizational skills, planning competence, networked thinking, flexibility, decision-making behavior, and ability to delegate.

With AE, virtual company environments, called microcosms, can be configured to test a candidate via PC-based role-playing.

The test instruments, for example, include the microcosm Home Robot, developed in MIT's Sloan School of Management. As manager of a fictitious high-tech company, the candidate launches a newly developed home robot against competitors. Thus a personality profile of the person being tested can be established.

The breakthrough for Habon was the Learntec in Karlsruhe, Germany, in 1994—a trade fair for innovative education technologies (sponsored by SAP) where Klaus Tschira became aware of Habon's test software. Tschira's vision was to fill a gap in the market for human resources software.

As a rule, the data managed by personnel development software come not from standardized sources, but from certificates or other application materials. Assessment software would allow the human resources department to collect personnel development data in a standardized format. Meanwhile, the R/3 module HR has an interface to the AE software. Thus, the data on qualifications can be stored and processed together with master personnel data and transaction data in R/3 HR.

An additional program is Team Up. This multimedia educational and diagnosis program focuses on team building and team ability. Digitized video clips put the user in the role of a consultant who supports a team—a journalist, a movie producer, an events manager, and a best-selling author—in establishing a private TV station on behalf of a group of investors.

The candidate has to interact within the group process, comment on the roles of the team members, and finally fill out a questionnaire. In combination with a computerized analysis of the candidate's behavior, this is the basis for the follow-up interview with the personnel manager. Team Up and Assessment Excellence serve not as substitutes for personnel development measures but as supporting instruments.

In 1995 SAP commissioned the software group to develop a system for computerized certification of SAP software professionals—what became ACE—and in the beginning of 1996 they founded AsseT. With 75 percent of the common capital stock of DM 500,000, SAP became the majority shareholder, and today the former start-up is part of the SAP group.

Now AsseT offers comprehensive services for R/3 certification, preparing the tests (in German, English, French, Spanish, or Japanese) to be used in SAP branch offices or at partner firms around the globe. AsseT also trains test managers.

Anyone who wants to be certified as an R/3 consultant must complete 70 percent of all test tasks correctly (though the SAP certificate is not a guarantee of excellence).

SAP's goal—and AsseT's—is that the SAP certificate should allow prospective clients to assess conclusions about the knowledge of R/3 consultants in industry-specific situations. More than 50,000 SAP implementation specialists worldwide have been certified by AsseT since 1996.

Chapter Seven

Corporate Culture—
The Beehive in Walldorf

E ven after ten o'clock at night you might encounter a long line of cars at the intersection nearest SAP's headquarters in Wall-dorf. On all floors of the building, lights are still on—and it's not because of the cleaning teams.

The IT professionals coming from and going to the high-tech citadel are not on an unusual shift schedule but are volunteers, either arriving in order to continue their work or leaving because they're done for the moment. Many of those just finishing up will come in later than the standard starting hour the next morning. And what does the boss say? "We trust our employees," explains Dietmar Hopp. "It's not only the bosses who can come in at eleven A.M." Smiling, he adds: "And we don't say anything when they're still at work at eight P.M." Helmut Gilbert, personnel manager of SAP, adds: "On Saturdays, too, many employees drop by."

"In comparison to other companies, SAP is a beehive," says Gert Goebel, a journalist with the newspaper *Mannheimer Morgen*.

The chaos pays off—for the shareholders, too—and there's actually more method there than it might appear. "It is a characteristic of all successful IT companies that they have an open corporate culture that promotes creativity," explains Wolfgang Fürniss, in charge of corporate relations at SAP. SAP engineers "have no job descriptions, no titles, no dress code, and no deadlines," observed *Business Week* already in 1989.

"SAP is so successful in global competition because we have employees who are above average in terms of qualifications and motivation, and because we were lucky enough to anticipate the future trends in data processing," explains Dietmar Hopp.

Success Factors

"SAP is an anomaly in pedantic Germany," noted *Business Week*. "In contrast to overbureaucratized IBM, the SAP founders developed a management style with a minimum of hierarchical structures." The SAP founders loathe bureaucrats. They regard lusting after status as a handicap. Dietmar Hopp arrives at the office in a station wagon; at lunch he sits in the cafeteria—often in a polo shirt. The drivers of SAP's success, according to Dietmar Hopp, are flexible organizational structures, a lack of hierarchies, and fast reporting from project and account management to corporate management.

Again and again—perhaps too often for a company whose market strategy and selling effectiveness are legendary in industry—the cofounder of SAP emphasizes that the company's success is based on luck, too. Hopp's modesty, however, is a personal trait that is acknowledged by employees, friends, and opponents alike.

He is good at figures and is a born businessman, but he tries to avoid the limelight. During public appearances Hopp seems shy. His reserved style influences how the company represents itself, too.

His motto is: "Keep a low profile. Too much uncontrolled attention could be bad." And at SAP snobbery is regarded as a deadly sin, explains personnel manager Helmut Gilbert. Anyone who does not observe this unwritten law is ripe for a dressing-down. In the beginning of 1997 there was a stir of annoyance on the executive floor at SAP because of a news agency report that Hasso Plattner had chartered a Qantas jumbo jet in order to fly in a reserve mast for his yacht, *Morning Glory,* for the Sydney-Hobart boat race in December 1996. Hopp made it clear he was anything but happy about this publicity.

It is true that Hopp proudly emphasizes the contribution of the SAP culture to the company's success. But at the same time the chairman—who also says that he has never read a management book—makes no secret that setting an example and comparisons with other firms do not mean much to him.

"The total social environment focuses on employees," emphasizes Helga Classen, an employee representative on the supervisory board. But the trade union still looks with suspicion at SAP because SAP never was a member of the German employers' association, there is no wage agreement, and employees do not have any formal elected representation within the company.

"Trade unions and elected representation have their merits, but there are firms that need neither. To that group belongs SAP," lectures Hopp.

The SAP model has nothing to do with cultivating harmony. On the contrary, SAP employees are proud of their disputational culture and the organized chaos that seems to be a guarantee of continuous change. "IBM painfully experienced what a powerful backward-oriented bureaucracy leads to," remarked Hopp.

The SAP model cannot be transferred to other companies or sectors of industry; SAP cannot be compared with Microsoft. Visitors to Walldorf can see and feel a peculiar mixture of universitylike atmosphere, sports spirit, perfectionism, chaos, creativity, globalization, and the kind of robust patriarchal management that one would expected more from a metal-processing company.

At Microsoft, employees pay homage to the youth culture in a way that has been caricatured in the novel *Microslaves* by Generation X author Douglas Copland. The microkids in Redmond, Washington, venerate Bill Gates as a high-tech saint.

At SAP, distance prevails. Despite the casualness that characterizes relations between SAP's other employees, the normal way of addressing the CEO is "Herr Hopp"—only a few call him by his first name. In spite of all the globalization, the fact remains that SAP is a German company. Speed and team meetings are emblematic of the working climate at SAP. "They work hard and unemotionally," wrote the newspaper *Frankfurter Allgemeine Zeitung*.

"It is difficult to find SAP employees or customers who criticize the company," wrote *Manager Magazin* in 1996. "You can only hear criticism if you ensure the strictest confidence."

On the other hand, the staff turnover per year is less than 2 percent, whereas software providers in general have a staff turnover between 10 and 20 percent.

Employee Surveys

Here are some facts about employment at SAP:

- SAP primarily recruits university graduates.
- As an employer, SAP enjoys a high profile; in 1996, eighteen thousand applications came into the personnel department in Walldorf alone.
- In 1997, the staff of the SAP Group grew significantly, rising by 3,654 to 12,856. The average age of SAP employees is slightly under thirty-five, with approximately four-fifths of all employees under forty.
- The average length of service at SAP is about four years.
- The proportion of SAP employees with college degrees is 85 percent; the proportion of employees with doctorates is 14 percent.
- Twenty-eight percent of SAP employees are women.

- In the spring of 1996 SAP conducted its first employee survey in Germany, the results of which were overwhelmingly positive. Ninety-four percent of SAP employees answered that all in all they are "very satisfied with their employer." At other high-tech firms the rate of satisfaction on average is 74 percent.
- Helga Classen, an employee representative on the board, explains the high job satisfaction as a result of the good social environment.

Compensation

One of the reasons for the attractiveness of SAP as an employer is its comprehensive compensation package, which includes salary, noncompulsory social security benefits (e.g., continued payment of salary for up to twelve months in case of illness), and profit sharing.

Entry-level employees with a university degree earn an average salary of $42,200 per year; new hires with a doctorate degree average $46,200. Cafeteria meals and beverages are offered free of charge. Sauna and sports facilities can be used free of charge. Anyone who travels on business more than 10,000 kilometers per year is entitled to a company car.

For employees building a house or buying an apartment, the company provides long-term interest-free loans. "In order to find another company that offers such benefits, you must look for a long time," says Jürgen Hachenberger, one of SAP's R/2 pioneers.

In 1995 SAP introduced a profit-sharing plan for employees. Each year the budget for salary increases is divided into two parts: one by which the basic salary will be increased, and the other half for the variable profit sharing that will be paid only when that year's targets are achieved. Personnel manager Helmut Gilbert estimated that this part of the salary equation could be 15 percent of the total salary in the year 2000.

Additionally, the company pays an individual annual bonus for special performance.

High Commitment

The reason for the SAP employee's strong commitment to the company is not only its good salaries. SAP also cultivates a strongly developed team spirit that is part of the secret of its success. To the unified, reserved outward presentation corresponds an unusually open internal culture in which employees fearlessly discuss and—often self-critically—make suggestions. "Confidence plays a central role in the corporate culture of SAP," explains CEO Hopp.

The SAP cofounder, who sometimes is criticized as incapable of tolerating criticism, considers total openness—internally, at least—as important for survival.

"In their internal relationships our employees developed a self-confidence due to trust and mutual tolerance that, in turn, is the basis for better performance," explains Dietmar Hopp. Weak points are discussed within the company but, according to an iron rule, not outside of it. That would be, so to speak, betrayal of the common cause.

As a result, the company seemed to be sealed off. This impression is reinforced through the characteristic SAP-speak that is sprinkled with cryptic terms and acronyms: "Internet Kanban," "ALE Web," and "work flow API."

"A special esprit de corps prevails at SAP," says Gilbert. This esprit de corps is mobilized not only when there is a need to protect the company against real or imagined enemies, but also in day-to-day operations. In a company where it is a question of million-dollar budgets for both customers and suppliers in installing hardware and software, foulups must be minimized, but they do happen. At SAP, however, individuals don't worry about being sacrificed as a scapegoat when a mistake occurs. The team takes the consequences together.

"Afterward, we don't talk about such mishaps anymore," says a young software developer. Sometimes, however, it's something to sing about, since the esprit de corps has even generated its own brand of SAP folk songs. This software company is probably the only one in the world to celebrate its programming errors in dark-humored beer songs. The "SAP Song," for example, celebrating the career of a carefree Badenian software hero, is usually sung at company parties in Germany, with no customers around: "And then he turns to pick up the phone: Why bother about data hash? Just let it crash."

Teutonic uniformity in thinking, however, is regarded as counterproductive. Hopp explains that the legendary IBM motto "Think!" applies at SAP, too—but in a modified version: "Think—but don't all think alike!" The main difference between SAP and the clumsy IBM bureaucracy of the 1970s and 1980s is that SAP relies on the sovereignty and professional competence of employees who do not hide behind the organization and do not try to cover themselves against each possibly expensive decision. The philosophy of the firm is that a shortage of commitment is worse than expensive mistakes.

Claus Heinrich, a board member, explains: "Let us assume that during an SAP expert's visit to a customer, a decision must be made. In most places the employee would need to go back to corporate headquarters and run the decision by someone—or even ask someone higher up to make it. But the management style of SAP promotes empowerment through trust in the employees. It is better that employees decide nine times right and once wrong than always ask the superior for a decision.

"The customer benefits from this attitude. They can count on us for competent experts who are committed to the task and make decisions independently. That is the core philosophy of SAP," adds Heinrich.

Principles of Management

"We didn't find our principles of management in textbooks," comments Dietmar Hopp. These are:

- Empowerment instead of control
- Committed employees instead of bureaucratic recipients of instructions
- Lean organizational structures
- Quality management as a common cause

"The management team of SAP has already put into action what elsewhere are only catchwords," commented *Manager Magazin* back in 1988.

Although Dietmar Hopp sometimes likes to explain that the roots of the SAP culture are in the open-plan office of the IBM branch office in Mannheim, the corporate culture of SAP can more accurately be compared with that of Hewlett-Packard.

Hewlett-Packard's founders, William R. Hewlett and David Packard, established their firm in a garage in Palo Alto. The "HP way" that later influenced numerous young firms in the first high-tech region of the world, writes publicist Anthony Sampson, is based "on the conviction of cofounder Bill Hewlett that men and women want to do a good job and that they will do that, if you offer them the appropriate environment. In the quicksand of Silicon Valley, that allowed Hewlett-Packard to withstand storms and floods and preserved its specific characteristics."

The characteristics of HP are close solidarity, informality, and a feeling of equality that manifests itself in the policy of open doors and calling everyone by first names. In fact, HP was regarded as a pioneer for a new style of leadership and a new way of motivating employees. HP introduced a generous model for profit sharing and established "management by objectives," which grants more elbow room to department heads and young executives. Another way of describing HP's leadership style is "management by wandering around," a phrase coined by John Doyle, then HP's personnel manager in Palo Alto.

Sampson writes: "Other large companies admired HP and asked which success drivers leveraged HP's top position. The secret easily can be revealed. It is primarily the result of the unusual continuity of the two men at the top of the leading group." With SAP the situation is similar.

Helmut Gilbert, SAP's personnel manager, likes to compare SAP with HP, because he was a personnel manager at HP before he joined SAP in 1994. "In some areas things are even more informal at SAP than at HP," he adds. "In the last years there has been a successful transition to the next generation of executives. The style of the founders has continued with younger board members such as Kagermann and Zencke."

The main difference between SAP and other large computer firms in Germany is that while a single entrepreneur such as Heinz Nixdorf, Friedrich August Meyer, founder of ADV-Orga, or Peter Schnell, founder of Software AG, had a formative influence on their firms, in SAP's initial phase its five cofounders and their crew already performed as a team, with evenly distributed and joint responsibilities.

Describing the decision-making process among SAP's cofounders more than twenty years after the company's founding, Hopp said, "We've never had serious controversies. If one of us had been passionately against a decision, we probably would not have made that decision. The characteristic management style evolved over the years. I think our strength was to pull others through by demonstrating performance. This pragmatic style also meant that the SAP cofounders did not get out of their depth."

Twenty-five years after the company's beginning, the founders of SAP can be sure that the elements of the SAP corporate culture are still in tune with their initial vision. But at the same time there are more and more signs that the SAP structure has to be adjusted to the rapid growth of the company. "With increasing size, the flexible company that functioned well in the past requires more time," wrote *Manager Magazin* in 1996.

It was practically unavoidable that some bureaucratic niches would develop. "Don't we already have 'public servants' for whom territory is important?" comments Hopp. In addition, more than 70 percent of all SAP's employees have been with the company less than five years—which means that the corporate culture constantly must be reinvented. "Meanwhile, we have software developers who haven't ever seen a customer," adds Hopp.

Dietmar Hopp points out four additional elements of the corporate culture:

- **Lack of hierarchies** SAP differentiates among only three levels of authority: the board, department heads, and staff. "Thus the performance of the individual remains visible, and it ensures that I receive unadulterated information," says Hopp. At SAP, developing one's career means taking on more responsibility, for example, in projects.
- **Open information flows and exchange of information** SAP banks on networking, encouraging its staff to establish an informal, personal information network. The better the employees are at networking, the better their chances of being promoted.
- **Flexible working hours** The contractual working time is forty hours a week. But, Hopp says, "our employees orientate themselves by their task and are free to go home when they are not in good form."
- **Continuous learning** SAP relies on lifelong learning. The employees decide to a great extent which internal or external training courses they will attend. They also have the option of shifting jobs within the company.

"Every Time the Description Is Different"

Meeting with Young SAP Employees

In October 1996 the author of this book had a meeting with the following SAP employees:

- Andreas Baader, age twenty-nine, working with SAP since 1996 as an assistant to the board
- Sabine Diers, age twenty-nine, employed since 1996 working as a consultant in the branch office in Hamburg
- Reiner Bildmayer, age thirty-six, working in product management for process industries since 1995
- Andreas Knopf, age twenty-seven, hired in 1995 with a position in the finance department
- Mirjam Sonnleithner, age twenty-eight, since 1994 employed in the DEC Competence Center (for coordination of development and sales activities jointly with DEC)

Gerd Meissner: What was your first impression of SAP?

Mirjam Sonnleithner: When I joined SAP, I had just finished my studies at the university of applied sciences and had no vocational experience—aside from jobs I'd held during summer vacations. I noticed that many people here are very young. I enjoyed the relaxed atmosphere. Now, I've been working in my department for two years, and my first impressions proved true. There are four in my department between the ages of twenty-six and thirty-five, and we work closely together. That's the kind of teamwork that I have in mind.

Gerd Meissner: Impressions can change after a while. What do you see more realistically?

Andreas Knopf: I had experience in a research institute. In order to change something there, I had to struggle hard with the bureaucracy. But the SAP system has disadvantages, too, as I found out. When many things are done very quickly, mistakes are unavoidable. Sometimes decisions are made in a hurry and later they say, "That was unnecessary." But you put up with it.

Reiner Bildmayer: I've been working as a consultant for fifteen years and have traveled a lot. I've seen many enterprises—but none like SAP. I like to come here every morning.

Gerd Meissner: So it's all paradise at world headquarters in Walldorf?

Reiner Bildmayer: No, there's always trouble. But it *is* fun. Other companies use sophisticated planning procedures, but it takes so long that before they can take any action, the opportunity is lost. Who needs two years for planning? In the meantime, the managing director puts you under pressure, causes quite a stir, and disappears. Here, it is different. We can plan calmly and can make progress together.

Sabine Diers: Here, everybody is asked to find his own way. You will have a chance to implement ideas.

Andreas Baader: I used to work as a consultant at Microsoft. There was a similar atmosphere.

Gerd Meissner: *Can everybody manage with so much latitude?*

Reiner Bildmayer: In the beginning, this liberty shocked me. I didn't have anything to hold on to; I missed having something to orient myself by. And all those training courses—that was a lot. To find out whom you should ask was most difficult. Here you cannot rely on hierarchical structures. It can be quite troublesome to find your way in this labyrinth. When new employees ask how the service area—where I work—is structured, we draw small boxes. But these sketches are relatively vague. Afterward they will go in the wastebasket. Every time the description is different.

Mirjam Sonnleithner: I think we're missing organizational structures that would offer a better frame for the team. By no means am I asking for bureaucracy—but less chaos would be okay.

Andreas Baader: At SAP everybody has to struggle against chaos. In the beginning, I thought we all serve a common cause. But because SAP is growing so fast and there are not enough employees, again and again you will meet colleagues who believe they have too much to do. The consequences are tensions.

Gerd Meissner: *Who has experience with difficult superiors?*

Andreas Baader: Not with direct superiors, but with superiors of other teams.

Gerd Meissner: *How do you handle this?*

Andreas Baader: You must try to present your business effectively, emphasize the common objective, and hope that he will understand.

Andreas Knopf: And sometimes you have to let matters escalate.

Gerd Meissner: *When you want to participate in a training course, do you expect resistance from superiors?*

Andreas Baader: That was a hot topic in our department. It is true that training is regarded as important. But there are areas where the workload is so high that employees can expect resistance if they want to spend the time on training.

Gerd Meissner: How is internal communication via e-mail?

Reiner Bildmayer: Partly it's too good. We receive so many messages. When I return from a business trip, there is chaos in my mailbox. Everybody thinks his business is particularly urgent. Therefore, it is difficult to find out what is really important.

Gerd Meissner: Do you spend much time with e-mail?

Mirjam Sonnleithner: Total internal communication is handled via e-mail. One of the last matters that is managed on paper is the vacation form. And that will be changed, too.

Gerd Meissner: But e-mail can be time-consuming—it can get out of hand.

Reiner Bildmayer: Yes, sometimes it gets out of hand. The board's already had to get involved.

Gerd Meissner: What part does the Internet play in your work?

Mirjam Sonnleithner: We all have access to the Internet. At present, R/3 functionality for the Internet is one of the hot topics at SAP.

Reiner Bildmayer: From my point of view the Internet is still too slow. You must have spare time—more than I have.

Andreas Knopf: Very often I surf the Internet. In my department we work with several banks. I inform myself via banks' and brokers' Web sites.

Gerd Meissner: IT consultants travel a lot. Are there higher demands on young employees?

Sabine Diers: Indeed, we travel a lot. But it is up to us. Anyone who is going to have a baby can work part time.

Reiner Bildmayer: Obviously that's stressful. But if you don't do that, you'd lose your understanding of customers. Tomorrow, for example, I have a meeting in Philadelphia.

Gerd Meissner: How do you feel about being a representative of SAP?

Sabine Diers: I just returned from Zürich. I attended a seminar with participants from sixteen banks. When I introduced myself as representative of SAP, they said: "Oh, the monopolist." Of course, I defend SAP on such occasions.

Gerd Meissner: . . . because it has advantages, too, to sail under this flag . . .

Mirjam Sonnleithner: Obviously you'll hear a lot of flattery when people learn you work for SAP. But I don't behave arrogantly. However, there are several people at SAP who behave that way: "I am working with SAP, I'm king."

Andreas Baader: Indeed, arrogance is a problem. For example, in my field a consulting firm is interested in one of our solutions. They are happy when they catch us on the phone. At present, we are in the stronger position. That can lead someone to take advantage of this situation.

Gerd Meissner: *How do you handle criticism?*

Sabine Diers: Often you hear about a particular application, "That doesn't run under SAP." But often the reason is that the customer economized on consulting or training, or he implemented the software in a hurry.

Another risk for the customer is the modification of our software or the development of proprietary software. If they keep on departing from SAP with the next SAP release—which doesn't take into account this special case—they will have the same problem.

Reiner Bildmayer: The balancing act is to make the adjustments so future-oriented that they still will work with the next releases. Often it is difficult to convince the customer that a 80 percent solution is better in the long run than a 100 percent solution that leads into a dead end as far as software development is concerned.

Mirjam Sonnleithner: On the other hand, the attitude "Take it or leave it" is the wrong strategy. After all, we will benefit, too, when a customer explains his specific situation. We can improve our software and can win the next customer that is in a similar situation.

Gerd Meissner: *The prevailing SAP-speak is a mystery to outsiders. Can the customers understand you?*

Mirjam Sonnleithner: We begin to think in terms of SAP applications. Then we'll meet a customer and ask him: "Do you have CO?"—meaning his cost accounting, not the R/3 module CO.

Reiner Bildmayer: You're right—we use an internal code, for example, "dynpro," "building site," "being under water," "ABAP," "to trigger" . . .

Mirjam Sonnleithner: It depends on the customer. You shouldn't frighten the customer. In such a situation, I'll say, "In the beginning, it will sound a little abstract," and try to simplify. We at SAP, for example, call a Windows screen window "mode." But my counterpart won't understand this term. Therefore I must call it "window."

Gerd Meissner: *What are the unwritten rules of SAP?*

Mirjam Sonnleithner: When somebody leaves me a voice-mail message, then I must call him back.

Andreas Baader: We call everyone by first names right from the start. And the office door is always open.

Gerd Meissner: *Is there any time when the door is closed?*

Mirjam Sonnleithner (smiling): That makes a bad impression.

Gerd Meissner: *Is there an unwritten dress code?*

Mirjam Sonnleithner: There are no guidelines. It depends on the area—for example, training courses or customer calls. Meanwhile, I look at the customer list. If banks or insurance companies are concerned, then I will wear a suit.

Sabine Diers: I wouldn't call on customers wearing jeans. But it can happen that we wear jeans in training courses for customers.

Gerd Meissner: *Have you ever had contact with a member of the board?*

Reiner Bildmayer: Unfortunately, no.

Andreas Baader: Almost every day. My boss is Gerhard Oswald. So far I have had absolutely no trouble with him.

Reiner Bildmayer: I am impressed that Herr Hopp sometimes walks around looking quite normal in sneakers and a polo shirt.

Gerd Meissner: *If someone called you and said, "We'd like to offer you a salary that is 30 percent higher, and you'd have the same liberties and fringe benefits," would you be interested?*

Mirjam Sonnleithner: I would say: "Ask me again in four years."

Sabine Diers: I agree with Mirjam. I feel fine here. I think after several years with SAP you get "messed up." Many older colleagues say that after that time it would be hard to change jobs and join a normal company. I hope to develop within SAP.

Reiner Bildmayer: Internal moves are frequent. When somebody realizes that a job is going to be free, he can apply for that position. The new and the old superiors have to reach an agreement.

Part III

PUBLICITY

Chapter Eight

SAP and the Media— A Critical Relationship

Hardly anybody can understand what is cooked up at SAP in Walldorf. Therefore, investors orient themselves by annual reports, newspaper articles, and opinions of customers.

—DIE ZEIT

March 16, 1995, was a black Thursday for Dietmar Hopp. The CeBIT computer show in Hannover was over—that year more than 750,000 visitors from all over the world had attended. But the magazine *Wirtschaftswoche* from Düsseldorf spoiled Hopp's pleasure about the successful participation of SAP in this computer show.

SAP had demonstrated its leading position on the world market for enterprise software together with many partner firms in a magnificent exhibition, and had been featured at great length by both *Business Week* and *Der Spiegel*. SAP registered 2,300 business contacts during the seven days of CeBIT. Many political figures came to the exhibition, too.

Dietmar Hopp smiled for the photographers, but he was not happy about the big fuss that the press was making. While the attention was positive for the moment, Hopp guessed the media might one day turn its attention to other aspects of the company's affairs.

Handelsblatt had commented in October 1994: "The success of SAP is threatened less by competitors than by its own market dominance." In the last days of CeBIT, uneasy rumors circulated among the SAP personnel that on Thursday, one day after the computer show ended, *Wirtschaftswoche* would publish a report critical of SAP's software. Even during CeBIT an advertisement appeared in which *Wirtschaftswoche* wrote both that "SAP is selling well" and that the software giant is "too powerful and too expensive."

Wirtschaftswoche's Cover Story

The first time a German weekly dedicated a cover story to SAP was not a happy occasion at SAP headquarters in Walldorf.

Under the headline "Software Star SAP," the cover showed a round black bomb with a burning fuse. With a shake of his head Hopp leafed through the article. "Never before had we seen him so speechless," recalls a close colleague.

Inside the magazine the report began this way: "More and more of SAP's customers complain of obsolete technology, high costs, and expensive implementation. Will it go downhill from here?" The report picked up the thread of the story in *Computerwoche* in which IT expert Karl Schmitz had denounced the complexity of R/3.

Hopp was perhaps especially shaken because up to this point the media (aside from *Computerwoche*) had treated SAP very well. "Hopp had tried very hard not to be in the press," Gert Goebel told the newspaper *Mannheimer Morgen*. But now Hopp was "in the media's sights."

Hopp decided that his countermeasures should have a signal effect on insubordinate journalists and rattled analysts. He responded with an advertising boycott against *Computerwoche*. He also had a preliminary injunction issued against *Wirtschaftswoche*, and began an unprecedented advertising campaign against the report *Wirtschaftswoche* had printed.

With such a strong reaction, however, the story received added attention and remained a hot topic for months. SAP's overreaction merely reinforced the image of a company that was frightened of the media and intolerant of criticism.

Though Hopp felt this was the best way to protect SAP's reputation, internal critics argued that it was bad for the firm. After cofounder Hans-Werner Hector left the executive board of SAP and was elected a member of the supervisory board, he strongly criticized Hopp's actions: "From my point of view, that was going too far. We simply must put up with criticism. It must be handled in a high-minded way."

Wirtschaftswoche is a competitor of the newsmagazine *Der Spiegel*. That was reflected in the cover story: "In *Der Spiegel* SAP founder Hopp ruminated about his heritage and hinted that the decline had already started." Hopp had told *Der Spiegel*: "If we don't retain our ambition to be the best, if we lean back, the decline has already started." This remark in the *Der Spiegel* interview from February 1995 became the peg on which *Wirtschaftswoche* hung its story.

"The high complexity of R/3 changed into rigidity," the magazine quoted Karl Schmitz, of *Computerwoche*, as saying. And Joachim Griese, professor of information sciences at the University of Bern, Switzerland, commented in the article: "The SAP technology is obsolete." Additionally, *Wirtschaftswoche* described difficulties and breakdowns in implementing R/3. The article listed the criticisms of SAP and R/3—translated from SAP-speak and enriched with suitable quotations—that so far had been published only in trade journals like *Computerwoche*. "R/3 is a relic of the mainframe era," *Wirtschaftswoche* quoted a management consultant as saying. They also printed a statement by a former consultant of CSC Ploenzke AG in which he indicated, "We had been instructed to advise customers to use SAP." Consultants from other firms gave their comments as well. Basically the article claimed that the reason for the continued R/3 boom was the fact that companies were afraid not to follow the herd. *Wirtschaftswoche* used another metaphor from the animal world, too: "Risk-aversive managers follow the trend like lemmings."

On the second page of the cover story was the assertion that the SAP "dinosaurs" required at least double the computing power of comparable products. And *Wirtschaftswoche* insisted: "Manufacturers such as HP, Sun, or IBM are not sad even though SAP expects a commission for each hardware deal. . . . In plain language: When SAP, for example, suggests to Hoechst AG that it run R/3 on HP computers, then a substantial commission flows into SAP's account for the intervention—often a tidy sum."

Even years later, Dietmar Hopp still gets angry about the article's "outrageous slander" of his firm. "He took it very hard," says Jürgen Steinhoff, a journalist who witnessed the situation while visiting SAP for a story in *Stern* magazine in March 1995.

On March 16, 1995, when *Wirtschaftswoche* published its cover story, Dietmar Hopp sent a fax to the editor in chief of *Wirtschaftswoche*: "I have had the pleasure of meeting Mr. Burkhard Böndel," the author of the article. "It was amazing to see that this 'analyst' doesn't know the first thing about our industry." However, on Böndel's tape of his interview with Hopp, the journalist from Düsseldorf did not introduce himself as an "analyst," and had not concealed that he planned a critical report. Nevertheless, Hopp's fax went on: "We will carefully investigate his sources and will send a professional comment to our customers." And Hopp called Böndel's statement "that SAP expects commissions for hardware deals" as "extremely damaging to the interests and reputation of SAP." Hopp asked the editor in chief to withdraw the assertion in the next issue of *Wirtschaftswoche*.

The Interview

When Böndel had originally suggested in an editorial conference that *Wirtschaftswoche* publish a cover story about SAP, his proposal was refused: "SAP? Not a soul knows them." Then *Der Spiegel's* article, including the Hopp interview, was published.

In reading the three-page interview, the *Wirtschaftswoche* editorial staff realized that *Computerwoche's* strong criticism was not reflected in the *Der Spiegel* report. Editor in chief Stefan Baron made a note on the copy of the *Spiegel* interview: "We should interview Hopp, too, but totally in contrast to how *Der Spiegel* did it."

When the Schmitz article was published in *Computerwoche*, Böndel immediately started his investigation. After a thorough study of materials from archives and files, he visited IT expert Schmitz in Hamburg. In addition, Böndel made appointments for background conversations and product presentations with many people at the CeBIT computer show in Hannover—among them managers working for SAP's competitors.

SAP itself eagerly responded to his request for an interview. Chief spokesman Michael Pfister recommended an interview with Hopp. After articles such as that in *Computerwoche*, interviews in major magazines such as *Der Spiegel* and *Wirtschaftswoche* could help soothe irritated customers and investors.

In the preceding years SAP had had mixed press in *Wirtschaftswoche*, but the magazine could not be called prejudiced. In September 1994 *Wirtschaftswoche* had announced in two columns "SAP: Defeat for Hopp," when SAP lost out to Baan for the Boeing contract, but in the summer of that year, *Wirtschaftswoche* had paid tribute to SAP's market-leading position in the United States: "The German software provider is very successful in the country where the computer originated."

Whatever SAP's expectations, the interview on March 3, 1995, was a real disaster—both sides agree on this. A tape recording documented the meeting between Dietmar Hopp and Michael Pfister, from SAP, with *Wirtschaftswoche* editor Burkhard Böndel.

Böndel opened the meeting with the remark "Now, this won't be as relaxed a discussion as you had with *Der Spiegel*." Then he immediately launched his first question: "Mr. Hopp, recently you told a German newsmagazine you have had luck in the development of your firm. Since you lost the Boeing order, does that mean your luck has changed?"

Dietmar Hopp described the meeting with Böndel in this way:

"From his introduction you could assume that he was on the attack." It is true the question was not phrased delicately, but Hopp still over-reacted. Böndel said later: "It seemed to me as if I had committed an offense against the king. After the second question, when they realized that I had only such items on my list, the atmosphere was icy."

For the following questions, Hopp steadfastly refused to provide detailed rebuttals of the customers' criticisms that Böndel quoted. Instead he characterized the questions as not professional or too general, or said that the situation being cited had been an isolated case. Both Hopp and his spokesman expressed their view that the actual instigator of the criticisms had been the articles in *Computerwoche*. Hopp later complained: "I am quite sure that Böndel had shown up with an already finished story."

The interview ended after thirty minutes as abruptly as it had started. Burkhard Böndel described it as an "icy end."

Michael Pfister remembered that he received a call from a SAP customer the same day letting him know that an editor from *Wirtschaftswoche* had been making inquiries about SAP at his firm and that the journalist seemed interested only in showing SAP in a bad light. Pfister later spoke with other customers whom Böndel had mentioned in the interview and whom Böndel had contacted. The contours of the forthcoming *Wirtschaftswoche* story soon took shape.

Pfister says that he gave Böndel a call shortly before press time in order to answer any other questions the journalist might have. However, Böndel describes the call as an "unpleasant dialog that clearly had a threatening character." The call did not take long. Böndel closed the conversation by saying: "I'm going to get off the line now. Read what I write in *Wirtschaftswoche* on Thursday." Then he hung up.

SAP's Response

"He lies. And we will hit back with the same toughness with which we have been denounced." Hopp was beside himself about the cover story in *Wirtschaftswoche*.

Jürgen Steinhoff, a reporter from *Stern*, remembers: "It was total chaos. I had the impression Hopp was the central character handling all questions and giving instructions."

How should SAP respond to the reproaches? Should SAP confine itself to legal remedies—get a preliminary injunction and issue a counterstatement? These actions could be supported by a letter-to-the-editor campaign and would have the advantage of not playing up the article unnecessarily. If they did this, the matter would likely be forgotten in a few weeks. Hopp argued, however, that SAP should counterattack in order to calm potentially rattled customers.

"We had different views," says Peter Zencke now. And Pfister recalls that he counseled Hopp, "We shouldn't do that because other journalists might declare their solidarity with the *Wirtschaftswoche* journalist." In the following weeks this turned out to be right. "For Hopp it was quite different. For him it was not a question of tactics," remembers Pfister.

"In such situations Hopp listens to nobody—aside from Plattner," confirms an insider. Dietmar Hopp had the final say, and he wanted public satisfaction.

When his cover story in *Wirtschaftswoche* was published, many of Böndel's German colleagues congratulated him on it. But there were also direct and indirect journalistic criticisms. *Tageszeitung* in Berlin offered Hopp space (headline: "I Was Personally Affected") to give his opinion on the cover story in *Wirtschaftswoche*, and he used it to write, "This article and the attendant circumstances, but above all the far-reaching powerlessness of the persons concerned, was a new, bitter experience for us."

At *Der Spiegel*, too, the *Wirtschaftswoche* story was skeptically assessed. "Certainly journalists often present facts subjectively and biasedly," said Klaus Kerbusk, who covers high-tech industry in the financial section of the newsmagazine. "But in this story the facts had been presented in too biased a manner."

On March 22, 1995, the courts granted SAP's petition for a preliminary injunction, prohibiting *Wirtschaftswoche* from saying that SAP expected a commission on each hardware deal of 20 to 30 percent in exchange for so-called advice on platform. On the next day SAP announced that it would give its view on the additional reproaches publicly: "SAP has clear hints that the author had no interest in an objective description, but fully intended to write a negative report."

Media people excitedly waited for the second round in the conflict between SAP and *Wirtschaftswoche*. The magazine would not swallow the affront of being called prejudiced. Editor in chief Stefan Baron, in turn, filed an injunction against SAP's claim that Böndel had planned all along to write a negative story. In the meantime, the legal department of the *Handelsblatt* publishing group issued the opinion "that it was legally justifiable for special emphasis to be given to the criticism of SAP. The press is not bound by law to provide well-balanced reporting."

Dietmar Hopp did not waste his time on questions of law, because he felt immediate action was warranted. When the *Wirtschaftswoche* story came out, the share price of SAP common stock decreased by 5.5 percent and that of preferred shares by 7.5 percent. As previously mentioned, the first signal was sent to the trade journal *Computerwoche*, the supposed root of the whole matter, when SAP withdrew advertising commitments of $560,000 and canceled a hundred company subscriptions. The magazine responded, "SAP supposed that we were at the bottom of the *Wirtschaftswoche* cover story. We had been punished for a publication from which we had no benefit. Schmitz's article had not even been mentioned in the story." *Der Spiegel* reported on the spat, noting: "The successful software provider SAP responds to increasing criticism of its products with economic pressure."

SAP's second action was to spend $105,000 on ads in four large newspapers, with the headline "Open for Criticism—but Not for Untruth." In the full-page advertisements SAP responded to the main points of the *Wirtschaftswoche* story: "We protest against claims that do not correspond to the facts. Please develop your personal view on the basis of our statements as well as the comments of business partners, customers, and analysts." SAP promised: "Additional rebuttals of the article will be provided in a comprehensive document." Later, Hopp justified the controversial advertising campaign by saying, "When we counter with verifiable information, 60 percent of the readers will say, 'You are right' and 40 percent will say, 'You're just inflaming the issue.' But we have decided to take action against the untruth." However, the advertising trade journal *Werben und Verkaufen* commented: "Answer via advertisement will become a boomerang" and would give the impression that they were quarreling about trifles. The trade journal concluded: "Through the frontal attack on *Wirtschaftswoche* via the full-page advertisements in *Frankfurter Allgemeine Zeitung*, the general public merely became aware of the monopolistic structures at SAP." And some observers had the impression that SAP—due to lack of legal claims—was trying to clear itself through unsuitable actions.

The promised document, "Clarification by SAP of the Topics Mentioned in the Article," consisted of fifty pages—including many letters from loyal R/2 and R/3 customers as well as hardware partners. But this document didn't do exactly what SAP had intended. In plain language: *Wirtschaftswoche* concluded that SAP's glass was half empty, whereas SAP responded its glass was half full.

The Conclusion

The conflict between SAP and *Wirtschaftswoche* was settled on March 28, 1995, when Dietmar Hopp met the magazine's publisher, Dieter Holzbrinck, and the *Handelsblatt* publishing group's managing director, Heinz-Werner Nienstedt. The spectacular controversy was settled out of court and without claims for damages.

By now, Dietmar Hopp was keen to limit the negative publicity fallout of the affair for SAP. And *Wirtschaftswoche* magazine had a very good reason as well not to further escalate its conflict with the software company.

This reason had everything to do with the most crucial point of the magazine's SAP cover story, the very reproach that had led to

Dietmar Hopp's infuriated counterattack: *Wirtschaftswoche*'s reporting that SAP received kickbacks from hardware providers. As for this point, the editors had not cared to mention that a mere industry rumor—which had not been verified—was all the magazine could base its reporting on.

"The foremost presupposition for reporting rumors [in the press]," *Wirtschaftswoche*'s own corporate lawyer now had to lecture the managing editors, "is to characterize rumors as such, in order for the reporting editors to dissociate themselves from the content [of the rumor]. This, however, has not happened in the *Wirtschaftswoche* story."

According to his internal file, *Wirtschaftswoche* was "lacking any proof for its factual statement against which SAP has filed for a preliminary injunction." Or, as phrased by writer Burkhard Böndel: "We've been taken for a ride by one of our sources."

The bottom line: There was literally nothing this crucial point of his story could be based on—neither journalistically nor legally. Other, thoroughly checked and balanced results of his extensive research, which had led to the massive "Clarification" campaign from Walldorf, were rendered worthless.

"[The kickback reproach] just made for a nice twist," recalls the former staff editor, who now heads a PR firm in Düsseldorf. Says Böndel: "We could as well have dumped it."

Chapter Nine

Outstanding Performance for Shareholders

At present, in terms of financial performance, SAP is second to none in Europe.

—MANAGER MAGAZIN

AP was the recipient of much praise from its shareholders, who called it, among other things, the "jewel of the stock exchange" and "a bright star in the stock exchange sky." And in the fall of 1996 the magazine *Capital* reported on a survey of 120 experts in financial management, who said they trusted SAP's CEO, Dietmar Hopp, more than any other CEO. Their opinion was confirmed by SAP's financial statements, which bore out Hopp's earlier prediction of record growth—and this despite the sharp tumble in stock price in October 1996. The newspaper *Bild* wrote: "SAP is super, analysts are dumb!"

In November 1996, for the third time since 1989, SAP was the winner of the performance analysis of German shares published by *Manager Magazin*. Moreover, SAP was the winner in a comparison of the top five hundred public corporations in Europe, scored by financial criteria such as return on investment, security, and growth: "With a golden balance sheet and an unprecedented share price development, SAP excels over all other listed companies." For the first time, a German company was the best-rated publicly held corporation in Europe.

Development of the Success Story

In going public SAP was presented as a "growth stock par excellence" by Wulf Schimmelmann, then CEO of the consortium leader DG Bank, who was elected chairman of SAP's supervisory board. "But the actual development exceeded our wildest dreams," says Dietmar Hopp. The initiative for the stock offering came from Hopp. "In going public we achieved all our objectives," he said in 1992. "It gave our employees an equity holding. We also could increase our public awareness substantially—with corresponding positive feedback for sales of our products. And finally, we expanded our capital resources in such a way that we are able to invest worldwide and to hold our own in a difficult market." Looking back, Hopp complains of the shortage of venture capital in Germany: "Banks are too conservative. In the United States it is easier for founders to set up a business." For German software providers it is difficult "to get on the track at all. We had the luck to develop our first product at a customer and were not dependent on loans."

If an investor had purchased a common share at the initial offering price of $426 and reinvested the dividends (after deduction of capital gains tax and without tax credits) in additional SAP shares, with capital stock increases and without any further investment, this amount would have increased to some $20,505 by the end of 1997—an increase of 4,767 percent. The sobriquet "the miracle from Walldorf" seemed entirely justified from a stockholder's point of view.

Between 1988 and 1997 SAP common shares achieved an average annual return of about 54 percent. However, *Manager Magazin* emphasized in 1996 that SAP shares were less suited for investors with weak nerves, on the grounds that they were "high-risk—not for

conservative investors." One of the reasons, explained Hasso Plattner in a spring 1997 interview in *Der Spiegel*, was that SAP's share
price was more dependent on the trends in the United States high-
tech market than on those in the less speculative German stock
market. "Our industry is the largest gambling casino in the world,"
he said.

Previously listed only on the German stock exchanges and in
Switzerland, on August 3, 1998, SAP became listed on the New York
Stock Exchange in order to strengthen its presence in the world's
most important IT market.

Ownership of SAP Shares

Even before it came onto the NYSE, a big proportion of SAP shares
was already held by United States investors. In 1996 about 29 percent
of minority shareholdings were held by institutional investors in the
United States—that is, investment funds and insurance companies.
These investors, supported by analyses by market research firms and
investment banks, can respond to technological and economic developments in the software market faster than private investors.

Out of a total of 61 million voting common shares and 43.3 million nonvoting preferred shares, in 1997 three of the founding
shareholders, their families, or trusts established by them held about
66 percent of the common shares and some 5 percent of the preferred stock. Of SAP shares in free float, the number held by United
States institutional investors such as investment funds, mutual
funds, and insurance companies was about 21 percent. By the end of
1997 German institutional investors held 29 percent. Institutions
from the rest of continental Europe held some 7 percent, while those
in the United Kingdom held over 7 percent.

With these price advances grew investors' expectations, too. As
the price increased, so did the risk posed by vague rumors, negative
press reports, and critical analyses. CEO Hopp admitted in a *Der
Spiegel* interview in 1995: "The staggering share price causes me

more trouble than pleasure." The German stock exchange journal commented, "SAP is a prisoner of its own success"—as the sharp fall in the stock's price in October 1996 proved.

Nevertheless, as one of the top thirty stock corporations that are listed as leaders in the German stock index, SAP's market value increased steadily throughout 1997. From a low of $124.12 on January 2, 1997, the preferred stock climbed to a high of $335.39 on December 8, 1997. SAP's market capitalization increased from $12.8 billion at the beginning of 1997 to $32.9 billion by year's end. As a result of continuous price advances in the first weeks of 1998, SAP's market capitalization grew to some $38.5 billion, ranking it number three among German stock corporations—behind Allianz and Deutsche Telekom.

Value-Based Management

As in previous years, SAP's shareholder value concept has gained broad approval. In a survey conducted jointly by Price Waterhouse, the Association for Financial Communication, and the Center for European Economic Research, seventy-five international analysts and investors ranked SAP among the top three German companies that most consistently applied the shareholder value concept. Other prominent examples were Veba, Hoechst, and Bayer. Moreover, SAP is a future-oriented example of how the interests of a company's different stakeholders (shareholders, employees, suppliers, customers, and local community) can be balanced.

Consortium Agreement on Pooling Voting Rights

When SAP went public, the SAP founders were relieved that no single investor had been able to purchase a large number of shares. As Hopp puts it, they were afraid of "losing freedom of action and flexibility." Hopp explained: "By going public we could keep our independence, and we were so well padded financially that we could start the development that today accounts for the lion's share of sales revenue."

At the beginning of 1996, the founders and their families possessed almost 80 percent of voting common shares. But because of the high German inheritance tax, which Hopp called "scandalous," in case of the death of one of the founders, his successors would most likely be forced to sell a large part of the block of shares to pay the tax, which amounts to 35 percent of the market value of the shares. This lowers the share price and offers an opportunity for a takeover by a big investor. "If I were to be killed in an accident tomorrow, my family would be under big pressure," says Hopp.

Hopp and Klaus Tschira opted for a solution that other German enterprises had already selected. In order to ensure the independence of the firm beyond the generation of the founders, and to save taxes, they transferred their stock to foundations that had been established exclusively for this purpose and which pay no inheritance tax because they are acknowledged as nonprofit institutions.

The annual dividends are used for philanthropic purposes. For example, the Dietmar Hopp Foundation is dedicated to fighting cancer, and it also has financed housing for senior citizens. The Klaus Tschira Foundation is involved in art, international understanding, and research. For this last purpose Tschira purchased, for $4.1 million, the villa in Heidelberg that had been the home of Carl Bosch, the natural scientist and winner of the Nobel prize for chemistry.

Tschira's wife, Gerda, supervised what the *Rhein-Neckar-Zeitung* called "the most interesting and expensive reconstruction effort in Heidelberg." The villa was developed into a research center and meeting place for high-tech experts and young executives. Close ties were established with the universities of the region—in Mannheim, Heidelberg, and Karlsruhe—as well as with the Media Laboratory of the Massachusetts Institute of Technology.

In spite of the fact that the shares had been transferred to foundations, the voting rights remained with the SAP cofounders. By means of a consortium agreement on unanimous voting rights, the common shares of Hasso Plattner were included, too, even though he did not establish a foundation.

Hans-Werner Hector also transferred a small part of his shares to a nonprofit foundation—the Hans-Werner-und-Josephine-Hector-Foundation—that is involved in AIDS and cancer research. But because he soon left the firm, the cofounders' proportion of the voting shares was reduced to about 66 percent. The remaining solid majority should guarantee that SAP's business policy will not be troubled by the "principal agent" problem (i.e., the conflicting interests of investors and the board).

The fact that the principal shareholders of SAP manage the business as members of the board ensures "that the interests of management and shareholders—that is, maximum return on investment—are congruent," commented the bank Sal. Oppenheim Jr. & Cie. in a study on the shareholder value of German enterprises. Shareholders' associations praised SAP's information policy and in 1995 explicitly welcomed the rebuttal prepared against the *Wirtschaftswoche* story. According to the German magazine *Capital*, SAP is one of the few companies that answer questions concerning the intrinsic value of business units, growth strategies, and planned acquisitions.

Growth Strategy

Analysts observed with special interest how SAP manages its breathtaking growth. Hopp and his team were rated high for SAP's growth strategy, strategic alliances, and focus on the core business. "Growth must not become an end in itself. The highest priority is to hold SAP on the solid course," said Hopp. Instead of making daring acquisitions, SAP confined itself to taking over specialist firms that are important for the R/3 course, making strategic alliances, and establishing joint ventures.

Investments in Subsidiaries and Affiliated Companies

With Siemens Nixdorf, SAP founded the joint venture SRS GmbH in Dresden, Germany, with a 50 percent share. It also acquired a 10 percent participation in the share capital of IXOS AG in Grasbrunn, near München, Germany, the specialist for business document software, and a minority of 25.2 percent of IDS Scheer in Saarbrücken, Germany. SAP took over Steeb GmbH in Abstatt, Germany. Steeb, together with CAS, was developed into an R/3 system house for mid-sized enterprises.

Since the late 1980s, investors had been speculating again and again about a merger with Software AG (SAG) in Darmstadt, Germany, some thirty miles from Walldorf, the second-largest German software provider. Though R/3 requires a powerful database system, SAP offers no product in this field. Therefore, in marketing its software SAP is dependent on leading providers of database software designing their products to be compatible with SAP software. Collaboration with Software AG, provider of the widely used database software ADABAS, would have strengthened SAP's market position because Software AG already had an extensive international sales network. In the summer of 1989 the German magazine *Capital* reported on such considerations, quoting Dietmar Hopp as saying, "The long-term objective should be a merger." While SAP confirmed the *Capital* report as "factually correct," SAG's founder and sole shareholder, Peter Schnell, brusquely dismissed it as "utter nonsense."

But in the mid-1990s the topic again was discussed between these companies. "This time, only the pricing prevented us," says Hopp. After the retirement of founder Peter Schnell, who was replaced by Erwin Königs (formerly CEO of Linotype Hell GmbH), rumors promptly bubbled again. But in February 1997 both firms merely announced the foundation of a joint venture. SAP holds a majority interest of 60 percent in SAP Systems Integration GmbH in

Alsbach, Germany. The scope of activities of this joint venture includes support for R/3 users in public administration as well as for banks and insurance companies.

Participation of Employees

In going public in 1988, the SAP founders intended that the company's employees should participate in the success of the firm by purchasing shares. This created additional incentives. Moreover, in 1995 SAP started to link a part of employees' income to the success of the firm. A central instrument in motivating employees was the convertible bonds that were issued for the first time in 1988.

This is the German version of stock options. In issuing such preferential rights to purchase shares, many United States companies enable their employees to participate in the stock performance of their company. The SAP convertible bonds imply the right to convert them to shares within a fixed period of time. The employees benefit from share price gains: If the company is doing well, the share price at the time of conversion will exceed the price paid for the convertible bonds.

For example, in 1994, SAP issued convertible bonds, purchasable only by employees, for four million shares at a par value of $3.09. SAP increased the share capital, excluding the subscription right of external investors. At the time of issuing the convertible bonds, the share price was $46.30 and the price of the convertible bond was $61.73. About 3,500 employees purchased these convertible bonds, which could be converted into preferred shares in September 1996. At this time the share price was $166.67. On average each employee purchased 1,151 convertible bonds. Therefore, the average total gain in share price was $120,786. R/2 expert Jürgen Hachenberger said: "This measure gives me the feeling that my work is rewarded beyond the normal limits."

Suspicion of Insider Transactions

The German Stock Exchange Commission and the office of the district attorney in Frankfurt, Germany, suspected that insiders at SAP had used their knowledge to sell their SAP shares before the price decline in October 1996. In May 1997, the media reported on these suspicions. Under the headline "Getting onto the Biggest Insider Case," the newspaper *Handelsblatt* reported that more than a hundred persons could be involved in illegal transactions with SAP shares. Under German law, such illegal transactions can be punished with a fine or imprisonment of up to five years.

SAP handed over to investigators a list of seventy-one primary insiders (members of the executive board and supervisory board as well as other top managers) who had direct access to share-price-relevant data. But a comparison of this list with that of the securities account holders showed that no primary insider at SAP had been involved in illegal transactions. So the list of the suspected persons was reduced to four "secondary insiders" (employees with indirect access to data that are relevant for the development of the share price). Those persons' transactions involving SAP shares during the period under review were analyzed in detail.

As a consequence of this incident, SAP reduced the number of primary insiders from seventy-one to twenty-nine. Hopp announced: "Fortunately, the suspicion that primary insiders of SAP AG had made illegal stock market transactions did not prove true." (Strangely enough, due to a translation error *The Wall Street Journal* reported that persons under suspicion *were* primary insiders, thus giving the impression that SAP executives had speculated against their own company. But the newspaper immediately printed a correction: "The four aren't members of SAP's top management or supervisory board, as incorrectly reported.")

Chapter Ten

The Resignation of Cofounder Hans-Werner Hector

The whole organization did not respect him.

—Klaus Besier

When Hans-Werner Hector speaks about Dietmar Hopp, the hurt pride and bitterness mix with awe and admiration. "We regarded Hopp actually a little bit as the 'father of the nation,'" explains Hector. In the same conversation he reproaches Hopp for having used "all means—psychological pressure and terror—to make his colleagues do what he wants. That was the reason why I decided to opt out."

When Dietmar Hopp gave his opinion on Hector's exit, he expressed himself no less emotionally. "I feel ashamed of him," wrote Hopp to SAP executives in a 1996 e-mail classified as "strictly confidential." "Never before was I so mistaken about a person. Therefore, I must admit that I failed myself." Hopp said that he had no explanation for "the disdainful way" Hector left the firm—"aside from that he must have felt pressure because he didn't contribute sufficiently to our success. At best, we could have still used him to welcome customers."

SAP managers sarcastically maintain, however, that he would not have been the right man for that. They mention, for example, the December 1994 visit of the then–United States ambassador, Charles E. Redmann, to Walldorf. The ambassador, who was interested in the use of R/3 in public administration, was welcomed by Hans-Werner Hector, who gave a disastrous presentation in awkward English. After that, Plattner advised Hector: "Play more golf. That will be good for the firm."

What had happened so that the former colleagues, after such a long period of cooperation, became fierce enemies who feuded publicly and washed their dirty linen in public? It had always been a tenet of the firm not to discuss internal affairs with external persons, but this rule was broken in May 1996 by Hopp himself, who in an interview with *Der Spiegel* attacked his cofounder personally, in a spectacular way. "Hans-Werner Hector simply does not have the caliber that is needed to manage a company. We didn't show that to outsiders."

The reason for this public outburst was this: Hans-Werner Hector, who possessed about 16 percent of the share capital of SAP and had moved from the executive board to the supervisory board, brusquely violated the understanding among the cofounders by selling a large part of his common shares on the quiet to a foreign fiduciary. The block of shares was sold later in batches. The dramatic move caused commotion on the stock exchange, rumors about a forthcoming unfriendly takeover, and negative headlines. "He always pretended that he agreed with the objectives of preserving the independence of SAP," says Hopp. "Then he sold his common shares and thereby trampled on our common objective."

Hans-Werner Hector confirmed that the "affront" was intended. But why? Dietmar Hopp at one point supposed "psychological problems" as what motivated his former colleague; internally Hopp justified his statement later as an attempt "to explain the unthinkable—and not with empty, diplomatic phrases that nobody takes seriously anyhow." The "public attestation of incompetence" (as one shareholder called Hopp's comments about Hector) caused observers to suppose that the reason for the rupture was a personal quarrel between Hopp and Hector. But actually the relationship between the other two cofounders who remained and Hector had been cool for a while, too. For years Hector was regarded as a fifth wheel on the executive board.

Past History of the Clash

Hector described his long-standing role in the founders' group this way: "I was willing to be a member of the team and do what was necessary." He remembers: "Tschira's, Hopp's, and Plattner's role was to think and to develop something new, and I was to help Wellenreuther to finish old programs so that we stay the course." In the initial phase, Hector developed with Claus Wellenreuther the DF system (integrated financial accounting, dialog version) and was in charge of batch programs. Later he did "those things that were necessary for the development of the module RV," the R/2 module for sales, invoicing, and shipment. Beginning in the 1980s Hector was in charge of SAP's training activities.

"By then, the stresses were already apparent," recalls Hopp; he would talk much less with Hector than with the others. Yet in the initial phase of the firm the cooperation of the founders had been great. That is confirmed by cofounder Claus Wellenreuther, who says that task assignment was never a point at issue among the founders.

Henning Kagermann describes Hector as "a team player. When there was a task, he accepted it." Hector said: "This 'duty calls' image actually accompanied me my whole life."

The terrific rise of SAP since the late 1980s left its mark on the relationships among the founders. When, for example, Dietmar Hopp fought with Hasso Plattner over the right course, "then the combat lines ran through the whole company," explains an SAP manager. But Hans-Werner Hector felt pushed aside on the executive board. In the meetings of the executive board, which were organized largely on the principle "Just come on—we'll have a meeting," they asked his advice less and less, and the sensitive mathematician increasingly suffered from it. "I had no say," he complains.

Primarily, Hector felt run over by the quick-tempered Hasso Plattner. He put up with it only because he felt obliged to Dietmar Hopp, Hector once commented. Klaus Besier, the former CEO of SAP America who left the company in January 1996, says: "Hector was treated horribly in the meetings. He never fought back." Hector admits that often they reached an agreement only because of Hopp's intervention. Ultimately, then, it was only because of Hopp that Hector still was a member of the SAP board. Hopp said: "Never have I had quarrels with Hector—it's unthinkable. He asked my advice, and as a rule followed my advice." This was so evident that for years a joke circulated in Walldorf that before a meeting one day Dietmar Hopp put thumbtacks on the seats of the cofounders, points up. The vicious punch line has it that nobody sat down except for Hans-Werner Hector, who said, "What of it? Hopp meant no harm."

At the same time Hector's management style frequently collided with the corporate culture of SAP, which is not based on controlling the highly paid IT professionals. Hector was reputed to scrutinize expense reports personally, even those of the most senior SAP employees. Hopp says: "Never in my life did I look at an expense report, but he enjoyed it. I told him: 'Throw it away and forget it.'" Several employees mentioned such incidents, but Hector comments: "I didn't think I had problems with employees generally."

The Turning Point for Hector

In February 1992 Hans-Werner Hector went to Philadelphia to run SAP's business in North and South America. Before his departure, Hector for the first time revealed his frustration to his colleagues. "If we can be fair partners again in the future, then I will do the job. If the cooperation is as unfair as it was before, then I will leave the firm after the America job and will sell my shares." Hector recounts that

Plattner answered: "I can understand if you want to leave, but I cannot understand your wanting to sell the shares." And Hopp told him: "You cannot do that. If you sell your shares, it will be a nail in SAP's coffin."

"When I went to the United States, I could barely speak English," remembers Hector. "It was incredibly strenuous. But today, I feel so good because I have learned to stand on my own two feet. I was right to do that. I realized that Walldorf is not the hub of the world. The years in the United States made me so strong that I could resist this psychological pressure."

So the conflict already was programmed when Hans-Werner Hector returned from the United States in February 1995. The business in North America had already become the domain of Klaus Besier, but now the business in South America, too, was withdrawn from Hector and assigned to Besier. Hopp justified this decision with the remark that there had been no progress. Hector explained: "The loss of this responsibility was the trough of the confidence crisis. Therefore, I said: 'No more.'" Moreover, the board refused to entrust the responsibility for the development of the new training materials for R/3 to Hector—instead assigning Hasso Plattner to take on this task, too.

In a talk with Dieter Matheis, CFO of SAP, Hans-Werner Hector let off steam. "For heaven's sake! I am fed up," Hector said, and Matheis replied, "If I were you, I would knock off working." Hector thought that it was a private talk, but Matheis informed Dietmar Hopp, who, in turn, took this occasion to have a talk with Hector that most SAP executives thought was long overdue.

Hector's Outplacement

Hopp remembers: "He had told our CFO that he would like to leave but didn't dare because he felt obliged to me." So Hopp told Hector in a friendly way: "You just returned from the United States. Before you decide to settle in somewhere and start all over again, I'd suggest you leave the executive board. You can move to the supervisory board." Hopp says now, "That was absolutely fair and well-meant." But the discussion that was intended to pave the way for an honorable way out ended in a quarrel. Hector remembers: "I told him that in that case, I would leave the firm—but that there would be consequences."

Hopp recalls: "The day after, he told me that I had fired him. I was totally bewildered and said to him: 'You are crazy!' I didn't take him seriously at all."

However, Hector was serious about it. He confirmed that he felt "pushed out from his position" by Hopp: "That was not only a job; that was my life." Hector never had expected that Dieter Matheis would inform Hopp about their private talk. He says he had expressed his annoyance due to "momentary anger" but that he "liked to work. After all, SAP was my child, too." Hector says it was a foregone conclusion for him that if he ever left, he would make a total break. But Hopp insisted that Hector should leave the executive board and be elected a member of the supervisory board."

On February 17, 1995, SAP announced that cofounder Hans-Werner Hector, a member of the executive board, had asked the supervisory board to cancel his contract prematurely due to "personal reasons." Hector would leave the executive board after the annual shareholder meeting in June 1995 in order to be elected a member of the supervisory board. A SAP press officer explained that Hector had "no plans to sell his shares." This announcement, however, was premature, because it took Hopp until April in order to convince Hector that the best option was a "soft" exit via the supervisory board. Backstage, lengthy negotiations with the multimillionaire started. Hector asked Hopp for severance pay and further payments to his pension fund—without success. A deep sigh of relief went through the firm when Dietmar Hopp spoke the (supposed) closing words for this chapter of company history on June 21, 1995: "Cofounder Hans-Werner Hector contributed much to the present success of SAP," said the CEO. "We thank him for all he has done for this company and are glad that he will remain closely connected to SAP."

Revenge of the Dropout for Twenty-five Years of Humiliation

But Hans-Werner Hector had made other plans. The words of thanks could placate him no longer. CEO Hopp warned the executives of SAP that it was not impossible that Hector would do something "unwise." Hopp says, "For him I was the evil one. To date, I don't know why." In fact, he did not think that his colleague would be capable of giving up the solidarity and community that existed among the founders. But Hector had perfectly hidden his intention, as Hopp sees it: "There rose a hate that he didn't show and that was rooted in his rather poor contribution to this firm." However, Hopp did not fear the worst until shortly before Christmas 1995, when a "bombardment of registered letters" fell on SAP.

In those letters, Hector offered his cofounders a chance to use their right of preemption for some six million of his common shares at a market value of some $1.1 billion. This offer was based on the average share price of the last quarter ($158.74 per share) and complied with the consortium agreement in which the founders had pooled the voting rights of their shares in 1988 on the occasion of going public.

The ostensible reason for this offer was that Hans-Werner Hector planned to transfer 0.78 percent of his common shares to his foundation and 10.46 percent to the Eugenia Trust, which was based in Jersey, the tax paradise in the English Channel. Later Hopp explained in an e-mail to SAP employees: "At this time, we couldn't have foreseen that Mr. Hector intends to sell his shares. But even if we had guessed, we wouldn't have been able to raise $1.1 billion without pledging our shares," because in April 1996, the Forrester report in which R/3 was assessed as a "museum piece" had depressed the share price.

After the offer, says Hector, someone told him that Hopp had remarked to his inner circle, "It is not necessary to buy these shares. For twenty years Hector responded to my psychological pressure.

It'll work out all right this time, too." With a triumphant smile, Hector says: "However, it did not."

When a new consortium agreement on pooling the voting rights of their shares was signed at the beginning of March 1996, Hector's former colleagues could not guess what he had in mind. The agreement was necessary in order to pool the voting rights again after transferring the shares to the foundations. In addition to the foundations of the other founders, the Hector Foundation and the Eugenia Trust joined the new consortium agreement. However, Hector made it a condition that he could cancel the contract with four weeks' notice but did not need to give a reason. The dropout would use this clause in good time—but he kept it to himself. Hector describes how he dealt Hopp a blow: "I canceled the contract on behalf of my foundation, and the Eugenia Trust sent a written notice, too." Hector gloats: "That really took Hopp by surprise."

"Perhaps this was his revenge for twenty-five years of humiliation," guesses Klaus Besier about the motive of his former office neighbor in Philadelphia. In any case, a stunned Dietmar Hopp tried to explain the behavior of Hans-Werner Hector later, when the Eugenia Trust and the Hector Foundation left the new consortium after a few weeks—without giving a reason and only four days after the new structure of the consortium had been published according to the law on securities trading. The message that Hector had transferred all rights to his shares to the trustee and therefore no longer had control over his block of shares, and that the Eugenia Trust had removed shares—more than 10 percent—from the consortium agreement on pooling voting rights, fell like a bombshell. At SAP, at the stock exchange, and in the press, everyone was asking what Hector's next plans were. His move shocked SAP's employees, too, who participated in share price gains via the convertible bonds.

In the press conference to present financial results on May 14, 1996, an angry and disappointed Dietmar Hopp appeared to still believe that Hector had made a mistake. "That was not very wise," commented Hopp on the transfer of the block of shares to the Eugenia Trust. However, he did not mention that Hector had offered to let his partners exercise their right of preemption. "We don't know what is happening in Jersey, whether shares will be sold or not," admitted Hopp. "The trust is giving out no information. Mr. Hector declared that he cannot cancel his transaction. We cannot understand what has happened."

If the six million common shares belonging to Hector were sold, this would considerably reduce the share price. Had that been Hector's intention? Or had he been cheated by a dubious offshore firm, as it was rumored first at SAP and then in the press? Also, there was speculation about an impending unfriendly takeover. Theoretically, an acquiring investor could get together a blocking minority of 25 percent if Hector transferred the remaining 4 percent of his voting shares to the trust, as the other 10 percent could be purchased on the stock exchange.

However, the trust on the island of Jersey was not at all a dubious offshore firm, but a part of the reputable Union Bank of Switzerland (UBS), which had taken over ownership of the block of shares according to Anglo-American law. The contract with Hector was made as a private-law agreement, so the trustee was not allowed to give information to third parties.

One week after that press conference, Hopp attacked Hector personally in a *Der Spiegel* interview, derogating Hector's entrepreneurial ability. "We covered him, dragged him, and never left him standing in the rain," said Hopp. "In return, he rewards us with this disaster." Nevertheless, the three remaining cofounders still possessed more than 60 percent of the voting shares and, therefore, a solid majority. At the end, Hopp repeated what he had already said in the press conference on May 14, 1996: "If he has character, then he will leave the supervisory board voluntarily, as my colleagues and I—that is, two-thirds of the voting shares—do not accept him any longer."

"Hector managed to damage the foundations of SAP," wrote Hopp in his e-mail to SAP managers. The other two founders left at SAP had the same opinion. However, the style of Hopp's attack in *Der Spiegel* was controversial on the SAP board. Klaus Tschira, for one, thought it was not a good idea.

At the end of May 1996 there remained no doubt: Hector was cashing in. It became known that UBS had sold 2.5 million common shares of the Eugenia Trust to big investors and had purchased 500,000 common shares itself. Therefore, the trust still possessed 50 percent of the block of shares—that is, three million voting shares. These transactions did not influence the share price. After a pause of six months, in spring 1997, the second portion was smoothly sold.

The showdown that was expected at the annual shareholders meeting in Mannheim did not materialize. "Today, the Day of Reckoning?" was the headline of the newspaper *Rhein-Neckar -Zeitung* on June 26, 1996. But Hector did not attend the meeting. Bernd Thiemann, chairman of the supervisory board of SAP, in vain had tried to mediate between the opponents. Now he read a letter in which Hector justified his absence with the reason that he would not like to stress the "extremely tense situation further."

"Until the annual shareholders meeting Dietmar Hopp had maintained that I had taken him by surprise and cheated him," wrote Hector. "That was not true, because I announced to him in 1992 my intention to leave if our relations could not be reestablished. And I repeated that in 1995." Hopp now declared for the first time that Hector had offered the right of preemption and that Hector's termination of the contract was not in violation of the consortium agreement on pooling voting rights.

One week later Hector commented on his own behavior in an interview with the newspaper *Die Welt*, explaining that he had instructed the Eugenia Trust to do nothing that might be bad for SAP or its shareholders. Hector did not respond to what Hopp had said in the *Der Spiegel* interview. Then, on December 17, 1996, Hector prematurely resigned from the supervisory board. From a compulsory announcement made by SAP at the beginning of December 1996 it became clear that at this time Hector still possessed 4 percent of the voting shares. The other three founders and their foundations had entered a new consortium agreement that pooled some 61 percent of the voting rights.

In a letter to Bernd Thiemann, chairman of the supervisory

board, Hector justified his resignation and reproached Hopp, saying the supervisory board of SAP could not adequately perform its legal duty to control the executive board because it was dependent on Hopp, who did not tolerate critical opinions. Hector declared in the letter: "I am disappointed but not surprised that Hopp through personal attacks tried to avoid a critical discussion of factual issues." Later Hector added: "In the environment of Dietmar Hopp, only those who dance to his tune can last long. All others will be slapped down, fired, or something else. Either they toady to Hopp and submit themselves to the psychological pressure or . . . The only exception in my opinion is Plattner. All the others, including me too . . . I behaved in the same way before I realized what the situation was." Hector claimed that Hopp had humiliated him because Hopp took it as a personal defeat when he couldn't prevent Hector from withdrawing his voting shares. But in the same letter Hector relented somewhat: "SAP would not be in its present situation without Hopp."

Hector wrote that the personal attacks against him had been "in contrast to the strength and competence of the SAP staff and the SAP products, in which I have full confidence now as ever." But the six representatives of the employees in the supervisory board refused to accept the justification for his resignation and urged Hector repeatedly "not to present himself as a representative of SAP employees."

Hans-Werner Hector was not invited to the celebration of SAP's twenty-fifth anniversary in Mannheim on April 11, 1997. At least one of his former colleagues would not have been against an invitation and even had tried to bring an end to the conflict. "I put him on the invitation list," said cofounder Klaus Tschira. Who had crossed out his name? "That's a good question."

Part IV

OUTLOOK ON THE FUTURE

Chapter Eleven

On Friendly Terms with Microsoft

It may be that SAP will not exist three years from now. But this could happen to Microsoft, too.

—PETER ZENCKE

G uests who visit SAP's development and sales center in Walldorf on a Friday afternoon will see a bustle that is unusual in Germany at the end of the week. Employees are extremely busy, and all the corridors are full of activity.

But on the second Friday in February 1996 the offices were half vacant and the corridors were empty at 2:30 P.M. The reason: "Bill Gates is coming." The message that the Microsoft boss was coming had lured 2,500 SAP employees into the cafeteria on the first floor. Since SAP had decided in 1993 to cooperate with Microsoft, the relationship between SAP and Microsoft had become closer and closer, to the point where CEO Dietmar Hopp had been asked internally, "Are we now married to Microsoft?"

Gates ingenuously affirmed that Microsoft had no plans to develop standard enterprise software and no interest in getting into SAP's market space. Rather, each company needed the other, emphasized the Microsoft boss, who praised the impact of SAP on

Microsoft's product strategy as bigger than that of any other software provider.

A year earlier, Hasso Plattner had said: "Microsoft is an ideal technology partner for us." The cooperation between SAP, with a sales revenue of $2.5 billion in 1996, and the United States software giant, with a sales revenue of more than $4.0 billion in 1996, paid off for both partners, and their customers benefited, too. Nevertheless, market analysts closely observed this cooperation. The top executives of SAP—especially Hasso Plattner—get along very well with Gates, who fits in well at SAP. "Although he is very successful, he stayed involved," said Henning Kagermann, a member of the SAP board, when being interviewed for this book. But many regard the boyish software guru from Seattle, Washington, as a brilliant strategist who does not believe in friends in the software business and powerfully pursues only one objective: to monopolize the world software market.

According to his own account, the computer freak duped IBM in 1980, when it did not yet realize the implications of the PC boom and so eagerly entered into expensive license agreements for MS-DOS, the operating system for PCs. Once Gerhard Schulmeyer, CEO of Siemens Nixdorf, was asked whether he would call Microsoft a monopolist. Schulmeyer answered: "Did you ever negotiate with Microsoft?"

SAP had several reasons for wanting to be on Microsoft's good side. First, Microsoft's network operating system, Windows NT, which could be used on different computer platforms as a substitute for Unix, plays a leading role in corporate data processing. Second, with its MS Office, Microsoft has a market share of more than 80 percent in office applications that cover word processing, spreadsheets, e-mail software, and graphics systems. More than 55 million PC users have installed at least one of Microsoft's office applications, such as Excel. Third, shortly before Bill Gates visited Walldorf, Microsoft had entered a new market that would influence all software products in the future: "The Internet will change the world," said Gates.

Microsoft, too, benefits substantially from the cooperation with SAP. In 1994 SAP acknowledged the network operating system Windows NT as a platform for R/3. For the United States software provider, that was a breakthrough in the sophisticated market for client-server systems. By then, Windows NT was in the shadow of Unix derivatives. But with this move by SAP, Microsoft was taken seriously as a provider of application systems for client-server computing.

In 1996 Hoechst AG, in Frankfurt, Germany, started an international large-scale R/3 project in which Microsoft became, after SAP, the project's second software provider. Through installing R/3 in combination with Windows NT, sixty thousand employees of the chemical giant would have direct or indirect access to SAP functions. The huge installation gave SAP and Microsoft international boasting rights, because Hoechst is regarded as a "flagship of state-of-the-art German entrepreneurship" abroad, comments John Pike, an analyst with Commerzbank in Frankfurt. Meanwhile, in an Internet variant of the event-driven process chain, Hoechst uses specific SAP and Microsoft software to connect different application systems internationally via the Internet—for example, to process orders.

Not only large industrial groups but also midsized enterprises benefited from the cooperation between SAP and Microsoft. Mainly in small and medium-sized enterprises, Windows NT, which can be used on both standard PCs and high-end servers, was accepted as the standard network operating system. In the spring of 1997, 48 percent of all new R/3 customers planned to install the software on system configurations that used Windows NT. As a database, very often Microsoft's SQL Server is used, and this had been adjusted for R/3. In addition, since the fall of 1996 R/3 users could analyze their data with Excel spreadsheets and can send and receive their R/3 mail with the e-mail programs Exchange and Outlook from Microsoft. Jeff Comport, a market analyst with the Gartner Group in Stamford, Connecticut, characterized the cooperation between SAP and Microsoft as a "natural partnership."

Additionally, the cooperation was strengthened by the fact that

Microsoft itself uses the R/3 modules for financial accounting, controlling, fixed-asset management, materials and logistics management, and sales.

Gregg Harmon, R/3 project manager at Microsoft, explains that Microsoft allowed SAP to control the transformation of the business processes—and not the other way around. It was, he says, "the most complex business systems implementation in Microsoft's history."

But what would happen if Bill Gates decided one day to develop sophisticated enterprise software, too, and to try to get his own products accepted as the gold standard for enterprise software? "The present alliance can break at any time," warned Dieter Eckbauer, who covered SAP for *Computerwoche* for more than twenty years, in the fall of 1996. "If Microsoft decides to develop enterprise software, too, then SAP would have a new competitor half a year later."

However, Plattner explains: "Microsoft sells application software, not sophisticated technology software, like SAP, and is looking for high volume. When we develop a new software system, it will total twenty thousand installations at a maximum." Nevertheless, Henning Kagermann confirms that "among our potential competitors Microsoft is the most dangerous."

In the fall of 1996, Plattner said: "If Microsoft was interested in developing enterprise business software, most likely they would develop a more global software that connects companies and companies with their customers." Thus Microsoft built Internet functions into its PC programs Word and Excel, and now you can load text files or spreadsheets that are stored on a remote computer connected to the Internet. Bill Gates sees the future in the Internet, whereas SAP plans to organize the standard software more clearly and to develop it into the leading platform for e-commerce.

Early on, SAP came to an agreement with Microsoft about technological standards for the Internet. The common denominator to which SAP and Microsoft reduced their strategy is business application programming interfaces (BAPIs). These standardized interfaces were defined in cooperation with Microsoft and were built into R/3 release 3.1 in 1996. The BAPI rules specify data exchange between different business applications—even of different software providers—that can be linked to R/3.

In the spring of 1997, more than a hundred software components that had been developed on that basis were already available. Too, the BAPI standard has had a formative influence on the new business framework architecture SAP has been using to shift to object-oriented standard software. R/3 components that are based on BAPI are in a way preconfigured and can be embedded quickly into the total system. Therefore R/3 users do not have to wait for a new release when they need a special component or updates.

Software Magazine pointed out that cooperation with Microsoft will strongly influence the technological characteristics of SAP software; in turn, Microsoft will increasingly adjust its product policy to the needs of SAP.

At the Sapphire user conference in August 1996 in Philadelphia, where the business framework architecture was presented for the first time, Hasso Plattner and Bill Gates showed how R/3 can be used with Microsoft software on the Internet. In the evening, the conference participants met at a party on the bank of the Delaware River. For this party SAP had engaged pop star Stevie Wonder, and the people from SAP and Microsoft had a grand time joining in on the line "We've got to reach higher" as the customers listened with great pleasure.

Chapter Twelve

Application Software for the Internet—Emitting Sparks

Perhaps it is an exaggeration to say the Internet is the start of a new era. But it means a new dimension of computerization.

—DIETMAR HOPP

A t the tenth annual Diebold software conference, held in Berlin in February 1997, Dieter Sinn, a senior consultant from Diebold, tore IT managers to pieces. "German IT managers are cowards." He heavily criticized their timidity in the face of innovation: "Though they welcome Internet technology, they do not turn to those areas that really count."

But Sinn could cite one exception in the German high-tech industry. According to Sinn, SAP has adapted its software to intranets and the Internet as no other software provider has, thereby accelerating the move toward e-commerce.

With release 3.1 of R/3 in December 1996, SAP became the first software provider in the world to offer a comprehensive application system that can be used both in intranets and on the Internet. Hasso Plattner proudly announced: "The total R/3 system in financial accounting, logistics, and human resources management can be used on the Internet."

As a further extension with additional modules—for example, for e-commerce—SAP announced R/3 release 4.0 for the end of 1997.

SAP's Internet strategy was praised even by those who otherwise criticize the company. So, for example, *Computer Zeitung* commented: "Again, SAP is the outrider." Even the analysts from Forrester Research in Cambridge, Massachusetts, revised their first negative findings, saying in spring 1997 that the open BAPI interfaces on which the Internet concept of SAP is based "are rapidly developing into the de facto industry standard."

Unjustified Criticism

Forrester's report marked quite a change. Just one year earlier, in April 1996, the same Forrester analyst had predicted that before long R/3 would be branded an unattractive, previous-generation product and suggested that decision makers be careful with investments in R/3. This earlier Forrester study, "The Prudent Approach to R/3," had forecast that SAP would not respond to the pressure of the market before 1999, but then would present a totally new software generation with components that could be flexibly combined and used via the Internet and intranets. "The facts were wrong, but the story sounded good and therefore caught on," commented Hasso Plattner.

In the 1996 report, Bobby Cameron and his colleagues from Forrester Research said that R/3's successor would be influenced by the intensified cooperation of SAP with Microsoft and would be built from scratch using a distributed, object-based design. It was on the basis of these predictions that they made the claim that R/3 would be "obsolete" within a few years.

The story caught on especially with investors, after the press reported the contents of the 1996 Forrester report. In vain SAP publicly affirmed: "Forrester is on the wrong track with this assumption." But it was no use, and the price of SAP stock dropped from its September level of $181.82 to $126.67. Dietmar Hopp noticed also

that a number of potential R/3 customers held back on their pur-
chases as a consequence of the Forrester report.

Bobby Cameron, who before moving to Forrester had worked for
five years at Dun & Bradstreet, the former United States market
leader for financial accounting software (and which had been over-
taken by SAP in client-server computing), claimed that SAP
had deliberately broken the first rule of the standard software industry: investment security for customers. "Companies that control
their business with SAP software are dependent on SAP," said
Wirtschaftswoche, hitting the nail squarely on the head. "The question whether SAP, as market leader, in time adapts its software to the
trend will determine how companies in the future can act on the
market."

Hasso Plattner recalls, "At SAP we were pretty much evenly split
over how we should respond to the attack from Forrester Research—
say nothing or take aggressive action against Forrester." By a narrow
majority the board decided on the second solution. Plattner remembers: "In resisting, we created publicity for Forrester."

On April 17, 1996, SAP gave a press conference in which Dietmar
Hopp and Henning Kagermann responded in detail to the Forrester
report. "We are not working on a successor for R/3," emphasized
Hopp. He clearly stated that Forrester was wrong, "because SAP will
not abuse the trust of its customers." Hopp confirmed: "We will offer
our customers investment security. We do not plan a radical reversal,
but R/3 will be extended in an evolutionary manner in order to use
new technologies—as SAP has done in the last twenty years." But
did this really count in view of the Internet upheaval?

It was not just the Forrester report that made clear to SAP managers in the spring of 1996 how quickly the mood of analysts can
change. For example, *Wirtschaftswoche* quoted an expert for financial management from the bank Trinkaus & Burckhardt in Düsseldorf: "All the steam is gone from the SAP shares." Peter Thilo Hasler,
from Bayerische Vereinsbank, who one year earlier had praised the
ingenuity of SAP in the newspaper *Frankfurter Allgemeine Zeitung*,
now complained: "At present, SAP's share price is less attractive

because price gains are below average." He went on to grumble: "SAP is lacking a clear vision."

Meanwhile, a new tone could be heard from SAP. It is true that SAP severely condemned the Forrester report, but for the first time SAP's response to the press showed restraint. Spokesman Michael Pfister explained: "Microsoft has bad press every day. As market leader, SAP, too, must get used to being attacked."

Henning Kagermann, the member of the SAP board who at that time more and more took over the role of representing the executive board in public, exerted a calming influence on those who regarded the criticism as a plot against SAP. On the question of what he guesses was the motive of the Forrester report, Kagermann replies: "An analyst's legitimate right to communication." By the very nature of their jobs, analysts serve as an advance guard for their customers, and their statements are often based on background talk and rumor. Where hard facts are not available, analysts can only speculate about possible trends on behalf of their customers. The Forrester reports, for example, carry the disclaimer that their opinions "reflect current assessments and are subject to change."

In fact, technical journalists with SAP experience did not follow Forrester's lead on SAP; *Computerwoche* pointed out that many rumors would come and go before applications of R/3's caliber could be replaced. Moreover, the Forrester report was based on information available as of February 1996. Experts on standard enterprise software noticed that, for example, the report did not take into account the BAPI strategy that SAP presented at CeBIT in March 1996. Even in February 1996, though, SAP had already announced that it would shape e-commerce in the Internet with R/3: "We don't wait for standardization, but define industry standards on our own."

As we have seen, some—including Klaus Besier—thought at the time that this was just marketing talk. On one hand, SAP could not afford to go into new software trends too early and too extensively, thereby unnecessarily making its customers feel insecure. SAP's cautious approach was indirectly confirmed by its response to the Forrester report. Peter Zencke explains that after the report came out,

SAP did a survey of its key accounts in Germany, asking whether and when they planned to use the Internet. The answers brought them down to earth again, remembers Zencke: "Basically, the findings were that we should never get involved with the Internet technology."

The Web Technology

On the other hand, the Internet and intranets were new opportunities that SAP knew should not be underestimated. Internet standards such as hypertext markup language (HTML) for the first time allowed data to be presented in a standardized way on computers of different manufacturers and performance levels.

Browsers such as Netscape and Explorer serve, so to speak, as a globally standardized "dashboard" that can be used intuitively. Through browsers, even high-end software—for example, enterprise software—installed on specific servers connected to the Internet can be used by standard PCs. "The first and most important challenge of the Internet is the opportunity to expand corporate information processing beyond the company borders and to customers, end users, and business partners," explains Peter Zencke.

This process was accelerated by Java, the new programming language developed at Sun Microsystems, and by its rival, ActiveX/VBScript technology, from Microsoft. SAP acquired licenses from both companies and thereby added two state-of-the-art Internet "dialects" to its own programming language, ABAP/4.

Java (the name is no high-tech acronym, but an allusion to the coffee consumption of programmers) is an object-oriented, open-standard programming language that can be used on computers from different manufacturers. In contrast to conventional software, a Java program is not translated by a compiler into the relevant machine code of the computer used. Instead, the Java compiler creates a "byte code" that will be translated into the relevant machine code by the interpreter (a built-in feature of the Internet browser) just at program run. This means the development of application programs that will be loaded and run directly from the network can be accelerated. In December 1996 Hasso Plattner forecast that Java "probably will be the future programming language for operating system routines."

Scott McNealy, CEO of Sun Microsystems, explains: "The Internet will change how enterprises communicate," because the new Internet standards increasingly influence the intranets. Using company software this way means that implementation costs are reduced; instead of installing and implementing specific client software on a workstation, for occasional users it is often enough to install an Internet browser. It also reduces training costs through the use of a familiar, standardized graphical user interface. And because Java applications that are updated on the server replace expensive program updates on the workstation, maintenance and configuration costs are lower. Two other benefits are an ability to use programs from different software providers, and increased integration and availability of programs and data through hyperlinks. Microsoft boss Bill Gates is sure that soon network software "will auto-configure, self-heal, and self-manage itself in very sophisticated ways."

SAP understands the new networks primarily as a way to expand the number of R/3 users. "It would be a mistake to believe that the Internet or intranet one day could replace R/3," said Dietmar Hopp. "But these are new communication technologies that can be added to R/3."

SAP Takes the Lead

The crucial impetus for adapting SAP's product line to the Internet came at a weekend workshop in Germany that was held in the beginning of 1996. It was a meeting of SAP developers and their colleagues from the Munich-based Ixos Software GmbH, in which SAP holds an equity stake and which specializes in document software for R/3 users. For Peter Zencke, the Internet meeting was "the best that we held in 1996. Never before have I seen so many sparks emitted."

Afterward, the IT professionals of both companies worked on "wiring" R/3 for the Internet, and developed scenarios for business on the Internet. Shortly before the CeBIT computer show the first BAPI interfaces were finished, and so at the show SAP was able to present this interface strategy, which had been developed together with Microsoft and had been coordinated with standardization committees such as the Open Applications Group (OAG).

Already in April 1996, the analysts from Forrester Research had quickly revised their findings and—just four weeks after the disastrous first report—presented a new conclusion: "SAP takes the lead on the Web."

In June 1996 SAP announced the Internet release 3.1 of R/3. Six months later—on schedule—SAP delivered release 3.1, which contained twenty-five application programs for use on the Internet or in intranets. "Our concept is that everyone who uses a browser can log on to an Internet server and use its SAP software," explained Paul Wahl in August 1996.

Now a standard PC can be connected via BAPI and the Internet with R/3, for example, in order to leaf through multimedia catalogs or to place orders. The industry-specific solution R/3 Retail, which was announced for 1997 as part of R/3 release 4.0, contains many Internet modules for handling customer-to-business transactions. Together with Intel, in the summer of 1997 SAP announced Pandesic, an e-commerce package that contains hardware, software, and related services and is especially cost-effective for small businesses wanting to make their goods and services available via the Internet.

Now via the Internet the R/3 systems of two companies can be linked. If a company runs short on materials, an order will be placed automatically on-line with the other company. Business partners, dealers, or distributors can use the Internet to ascertain current inventory, have a look at current price lists, or inquire about the status of an order. Moreover, encoded financial data can be exchanged in business-to-business relations via the Internet.

But we are just at the beginning of e-commerce. So far, neither in the United States nor in Europe has the forecast sales volume for on-line shopping been achieved. On the other hand, for most large enterprises the intranets have proved a success for reducing costs and improving access to information.

Specific R/3 applications have been developed by SAP for the intranet—for example, employee self-service. This concept allows employees to perform specific functions of personnel management on their own PC. At SAP, employees can open their personnel file via an intranet component of the R/3 module HR (human resources management) in order to check, change, or add address data; record a new member of the family; fill in a vacation request form; ask for a pay slip; or print out statements on any of the above items.

That the self-service concept is a success is shown by the boom in on-line banking. SAP assumes that the self-service concept will gain acceptance at public authorities such as utilities, too.

Epilogue

The company has simply woken up to the fact that the
United States are our most important market by far.

—Henning Kagermann, cochairman/CEO
of SAP's executive board

Over the past decade, the ritual at SAP's annual stockholder meetings had been pretty much the same. Fervently, the delegates of various shareholder associations competed to deliver the most impassioned address. With colorful metaphors, enraptured speakers hailed SAP and its leaders, praising them, for example, as the "four-leaf clover of entrepreneurs."

This time, it was different. At the 1998 meeting in Mannheim, just across the Rhine River from Heidelberg, a somber mood prevailed. The convention in May marked the end of an era at SAP. Earlier that spring, Dietmar Hopp had announced that he would step back from the day-to-day operations of the company he had cofounded twenty-six years before and become chairman of SAP's supervisory board.

"Often corporate crisis results from delayed or badly organized leadership changes," Hopp stated in a letter to SAP's employees and management. "At SAP, we want to avoid that risk." The reserved

Badenian, whose no-nonsense manners and earthy dialect blends in well with the Mittelstand folks in the company's home region, had been the business mastermind behind this unique German success story. His message left not only Walldorf stunned.

It also resonated in Silicon Valley, where many of SAP's customers and partners are based. "Even I was taken by surprise," says Heinz Roggenkemper, who started SAP America in 1988 and now heads SAP Labs, the R&D facility in Palo Alto. German analysts and the business press were equally puzzled, perhaps best illustrated by the picture accompanying a story in *Manager Magazin,* the monthly business publication from Hamburg.

The magazine wanted to show SAP's cofounders Hopp and Plattner with their candidate of choice to replace Dietmar Hopp and lead the company into the twenty-first century. But as the successor was no more of a publicity-eager corporate poster boy than the predecessor, the magazine wasn't able to come up with a photo that showed the three of them together. So they simply faked it. The business monthly printed a poorly manipulated photograph. It showed the new guy on a company construction site, mounted (as indicated in small print on the following page) in between the two tough-looking cofounders, smiling boyishly over their shoulders like the new kid on the block that has finally been allowed into the sandbox.

Nothing was farther from the truth. Company and industry insiders knew that Henning Kagermann had been in the picture for quite some time and had occasionally been described by SAP veterans as "heir apparent" of Dietmar Hopp. The mathematician and physicist, who was appointed to a professorial chair in 1980 and left a stellar academic career to join the company in 1982, was appointed to SAP's board in 1991. He took charge of R/3 development—financial and accounting applications, industry solutions, and international business—as well as of the European region management, excluding Germany.

"Quietly making a difference"—that's how the influential German daily newspaper *Welt* once described Kagermann. The father of three comes across as modest and diplomatic, but he is not reluctant to—always politely—voice his opinion. When cofounders Hopp and Plattner, who are known to have never been close personal friends, clashed heavily behind closed boardroom doors, Kagermann, according to witnesses, often sided with Plattner, whose "extreme talent to motivate people" he admires.

Like his predecessor Dietmar Hopp, Kagermann is comfortable with aiming high by lying low. Asked shortly after taking over his new position at the helm of SAP about his role as the first CEO who doesn't come from the group of the original founders, Kagermann said, "I see no use in worrying about someone saying someday, 'My God, these footprints were pretty large for such small feet to step in.'" Concerning himself with such matters, adds Kagermann, "would certainly not be my personal style."

Kagermann was the driving force behind SAP's listing of its preferred shares on the New York Stock Exchange, which finally took place on August 3, 1998. Joining other big players from Germany like Daimler-Benz, Deutsche Telekom, Hoechst, and VEBA on the Big Board was celebrated with a lively "beach party" on Wall Street. SAP shares (ticker symbol: SAP) are traded in the form of American Depositary Receipts (ADRs). Twelve ADRs equal one SAP preferred share. "Many of our investors are U.S. based," states Kagermann in defense of the NYSE listing, "as well as most of our competitors and a very large share of our customers. That's something one should't underestimate. Quite frankly, it's about visibility."

During the following months, the company got more visibility in the U.S. business press than it had wished for, due to spectacular changes in the top management of SAP America. Shortly after the New York bash, SAP announced that CEO Paul Wahl would leave its American branch after accepting an offer to head TriStrata, a security software company based in Redwood Shores, California. Kevin McKay, who had joined the company in 1995 as CFO, was appointed CEO.

Then, in March 1999, Jeremy Coote, after ten years at SAP's U.S. unit, joined Siebel Systems (San Mateo, California) as vice president of North American Operations. The company, a maker of so-called sales force automation software that helps businesses run their sales, marketing, and customer-service operations based on Internet technology, has emerged as one of SAP's fiercest competitors. And it was considered another coup when Siebel announced in May 1999 that Coote would be joined at his new company by an old buddy, Paul Wahl, who was named Siebel's president and chief operating officer.

Back in Walldorf, Kagermann will be measured by how he masters redefining SAP's business model for the era of e-commerce. In March 1999, the company put a colorful new face on its software, created by frogdesign, the creative powerhouse (Altensteig, Germany/New York/Sunnyvale/San Francisco) founded by German high-tech visioneer Hartmut Esslinger. Through the new graphical user interface, named EnjoySAP, which includes a new interaction design for accessing R/3's myriad of functions, SAP hopes to reduce implementation times and training expenses.

The battle for the Internet has only just begun. When this book went to print, it was too early to judge whether MySAP.com (see Preface) and EnjoySAP are marking an effective shift from a client-server software provider toward a true Internet company or whether they are merely clever marketing labels that will be dumped and forgotten within two or three years.

Kagermann did not learn the business in IBM's famous industry boot camp. Regardless of the recent dot.com craze, some rules haven't changed since the old days. "You don't have to be the Number One in coming up with new ideas, if you're the market leader with such a big customer base as the one we have," he says.

However the Internet may change the ERP industry landscape over the coming years, SAP, as a global company, has the means to remain a force to be reckoned with. As Kagermann points out, "We're self-confident enough that once we've seen the importance of a new idea, we get moving better and faster than others."

Sources and Acknowledgments

The author relied on many interviews transcribed from tape. He met the five cofounders of SAP—Hans-Werner Hector, Dietmar Hopp, Professor Dr. h.c. Hasso Plattner, Dr. h.c. Klaus Tschira, and Dr. Claus Wellenreuther—as well as members of their families; board members such as Dr. Claus Heinrich, Professor Dr. Henning Kagermann, Gerhard Oswald, Dr. Peter Zencke, and Paul Wahl; current and former managers and employees, including Klaus Besier, former CEO of SAP America, Helga Classen, deputy chairwoman of the advisory board as representative of the employees, Paul Neugart, sales manager for Germany, and Ulrich Daub, head of the corporate NCR alliance management; and fellows, competitors, critics, and journalists, including Professor Dr. August-Wilhelm Scheer, Jan Baan, Dieter Eckbauer, Dr. Karl Schmitz, and Burkhard Böndel. Helpful as well was a tape interview with Dr. h.c. Klaus Tschira that was made available by the journalist Achim Born.

The author thanks all named and unnamed interlocutors who contributed to this book with their information. Moreover, articles on enterprise software and SAP in the following newspapers and magazines were consulted: *Berliner Morgenpost, Börsen-Zeitung, Business Week, Capital, CIO, Computerwoche, Computer Zeitung, c't, Datamation, Der Spiegel, Die Welt, Die Woche, Die Zeit, Financial Times, Forbes, Fortune, Frankfurter Allgemeine Zeitung, Handelsblatt, Information Week, Manager Magazin, Mannheimer Morgen, Rhein-Neckar-Zeitung, Software Magazine, Stern, Süddeutsche Zeitung, Wall Street*

Journal, and *Wirtschaftswoche.* Publications of the towns of Walldorf, Wiesloch, and Östringen were helpful, too, as well as the video movie *Astorstadt Walldorf* (I. D. Medienhaus, Walldorf). Additionally, several SAP publications such as memos, e-mail circulars, the magazine for employees, video movies, and annual reports as well as the company magazine *SAP Info* were used as sources of information.

For those cases in which we did quote without an explicit source for the benefit of readability, the author begs the relevant writers and their editorial staff for understanding. Special thanks go to the journalists of *Der Spiegel, Wirtschaftswoche, Computerwoche,* and *Computer Zeitung,* the editors for business and local affairs as well as the keeper of the records of the *Rhein-Neckar-Zeitung,* and the *Mannheimer Morgen,* and to the employees of the corporate communications department of SAP AG.

The fast-moving character of the software industry is proverbial. Details on firms, persons, and positions are as of April 1, 1997, if not otherwise noted.

The author thanks all who contributed with their support in writing this book and whose names could not or must not be mentioned here.

Appendix A: Company History

1972: In April 1972 the former IBM system engineers Dietmar Hopp, Hans-Werner Hector, Hasso Plattner, Klaus Tschira, and Claus Wellenreuther established the firm Systemanalyse Programmentwicklung (i.e., System Analysis and Program Development) as a company constituted under German civil law. The registered office was in Weinheim, and the business office was located in Mannheim. SAP's first assignment, placed by the nylon fiber works of ICI, was the development of a financial accounting system. At the end of the first financial year, the firm had nine employees and the sales revenue was $194,400 (DM 620,000).

1976: As a sales and support company, the SAP GmbH Systeme, Anwendungen, Produkte in der Datenverarbeitung (i.e., Systems, Applications, and Products for Data Processing) was established. The civil-code company was wound up five years later. In the fifth year SAP had twenty-five employees and the sales revenue was $1.5 million (DM 3.8 million).

1977: The registered office was transferred from Weinheim to Walldorf. SAP managed to win two large companies in Austria as customers: the paper factory in Nettingsdorf and OKA in Linz.

1979: SAP started to develop R/2, the second-generation software for mainframe computing. SAP's first office building was built in the industrial area in Walldorf. In the spring, SAP's first data processing center was put into operation—still in rented rooms. The sales revenue was about $5.5 million (DM 10 million).

1980: The firm moved to the new building in Walldorf. The company had seventy-seven employees. Fifty of the top one hundred German industrial enterprises were customers of SAP. The contract with ADV/Orga for joint distribution was canceled. SAP cofounder Claus Wellenreuther left the company for health reasons with compensation of $550,000 (DM 1 million).

1982: The development of R/2—the system for mainframe computing—was completed. SAP hired its one hundredth employee. The sales revenue increased by 48 percent to $10 million (DM 24.2 million). SAP software was used by 236 companies in Germany, Austria, and Switzerland.

1983: New buildings were constructed. The sales revenue increased by 45 percent to $18.3 million (DM 46.7 million).

1984: In fall 1984 SAP (International) AG was established in Biel, Switzerland, to take on foreign business. At the end of 1984, SAP had 163 employees.

1985: The SAP data processing center had three IBM mainframe computers and one Siemens mainframe computer. Companies in Austria, the Benelux countries, Canada, Denmark, Italy, Kuwait, South Africa, Spain, Switzerland, Trinidad, the United Kingdom, and the United States used SAP software.

1986: SAP raised its subscribed capital from $230,000 (DM 0.5 million) to $2.3 million (DM 5 million). For the first time, the company was an exhibitor at the computer show CeBIT in Hannover. In Austria, SAP Österreich GmbH was established. In Germany, SAP established a branch office in Ratingen, near Düsseldorf. In Walldorf, an IBM mainframe computer with 64 MB of main memory was installed—an investment of about $3.2 million (DM 7 million). The sales revenue exceeded $46.1 million (DM 100 million).

1987: In March SAP started to build its first international training center. SAP established firms in five European countries. Branch offices were opened in Hamburg and Munich. SAP software was used by 850 companies—of which sixty belonged to the top hundred industrial enterprises in Germany. SAP had 750 employees, and the sales revenue was $136 million (DM 245 million). SAP started developing R/3, the third-generation software for client-server computing.

1988: The corporate legal form was changed into a stock corporation in August 1988. In October, SAP was listed on the stock exchange in Germany. Stock exchange trading started in Frankfurt and Stuttgart on November 4, 1988. The international distribution network was extended by establishing new firms in Denmark, Sweden, Italy, and the United States, where SAP started with SAP North America, Inc., in Philadelphia. SAP established a joint venture with the consulting firm Arthur Andersen & Co. The international training center was opened.

1989: In June there was the first general meeting of shareholders, in Karlsruhe. The international training center had to be expanded because the demand for SAP training substantially increased. Meanwhile, SAP (International) AG in Biel coordinated subsidiaries in twelve countries—most recently in Canada, Singapore, and Australia. The company had more than 1,250 customers and 1,000 employees. The budget for R & D was $44.3 million (DM 83.3 million).

1990: The subscribed capital was increased by issuing preferred stock in the amount of $52.6 million (DM 85 million). The economic and monetary union with the GDR and the reunification of Germany opened the market in the former East Germany. SAP established a branch office in Berlin and SRS in Dresden as a joint venture with Siemens Nixdorf and Robotron. The equity capital was $238.8 million (DM 386 million) and the sales revenue was $309.4 million (DM 500 million). SAP spent $67.4 million (DM 109 million) for R & D. The workforce was 1,700.

1991: For the first time SAP software was implemented in Japan. SAP software was used by 2,225 customers in 31 countries. The sales revenue increased by more than 40 percent to $425.9 million (DM 707 million). The company had 2,500 employees. SAP expanded the managing board: In the beginning of 1991 Henning Kagermann was appointed a member of the board, followed in April 1992 by Hans Schlegel.

1992: The development of R/3—the system for client-server computing—was finished. After a pilot phase the new system was shipped. The new development and sales center was opened. Now foreign business was controlled from Walldorf. The subscribed capital was increased by $9.6 million (DM 15 million), to a total of $64 million (DM 100 million), by issuing 300,000 preferred shares.

1993: SAP entered into a cooperation agreement with Microsoft. For the first time sales revenue exceeded $606 million (DM 1 billion)

1994: In November IBM bought R/3—then the largest order in SAP history. With more than 4,000 customers and a sales revenue of $1.1 billion (DM 1.8 billion), SAP was the leading provider of enterprise software worldwide. International competition intensified: In competitive bidding for the United States aircraft manufacturer Boeing, SAP lost against Baan, from the Netherlands.

1995: Hans-Werner Hector left the managing board and was elected a member of the advisory board. In the spring SAP defended itself against negative press reports with an advertising boycott, legal actions, and a press campaign. The United States software giant Microsoft decided on R/3 as its application system for financial accounting. In September SAP was included in the DAX (the German stock index). A new branch was established in China. The year ended with the largest order in company history: Deutsche Telekom ordered R/3 to be used in 30,000 jobs. R/3 was SAP's best-selling item. The sales revenue was $1.9 billion (DM 2.7 billion).

1996: In January Klaus Besier, CEO of SAP America, left the company. The executive board was expanded by three deputy members: Claus Heinrich, Gerhard Oswald, and Paul Wahl, who succeeded Klaus Besier in the United States. Bill Gates visited SAP in Germany. In May there was a rupture between SAP and its cofounder Hans-Werner Hector when they found out that he had transferred SAP common shares to UBS International Trustees Ltd. (Jersey). In October, a plunge in SAP's share price shocked investors: SAP temporarily lost $4.7 billion (DM 7 billion) market value. But later, SAP could announce the best last quarter of its history. In December SAP started to deliver R/3 release 3.1—the first enterprise software with

Internet and intranet functionality. In 1996 sales revenue increased by 38 percent to $2.5 billion (DM 3.7 billion). SAP managed to win 1,089 new R/3 customers. Worldwide, there were about 9,000 R/3 installations. The company employed 9,200 people.

1997: In February SAP found out that Hans-Werner Hector had sold a large part of his remaining common shares. SAP AG and Software AG, another high-ranking German software provider, established a joint venture in Alsbach, Germany: SAP Systems Integration GmbH (SAP-SI). On April 11 SAP celebrated its twenty-fifth anniversary. The ceremonial address was given by German chancellor Helmut Kohl. The workforce increased by 40 percent, to 12,856. With a 62 percent increase in sales, to $3.5 billion (DM 6.0 billion), SAP considerably exceeded the previous year's growth rate of 38 percent. SAP's market capitalization increased from $12.8 billion at the beginning of 1997 to $32.9 billion at the end of 1997.

- **Number of SAP installations** More than two million users work with over 13,400 R/3 installations worldwide, while some 1,400 companies use the mainframe system R/2.
- **Software generations**
  - **R/2 system for mainframe computers** The latest software versions are R/2 release 6.0 and 6.1. SAP will continue to enhance, maintain, and support the R/2 system up to the year 2004.
  - **R/3 release 3.1 for client-server computing** SAP was the first software provider to market a business application software package offering Internet functionality for a broad spectrum of R/3 system business processes.
  - **R/3 release 4.0 for client-server computing** This system—delivered in December 1997—is regarded as the most advanced and comprehensive enterprise software solution available on the market. R/3 release 4.0, focusing on value chain innovation, supports the entire process chain, from procurement and manufacturing to selling. For simpler and more efficient implementation of R/3, SAP

developed ASAP (AcceleratedSAP). SAP restructured the R/3 system into a portfolio of integrated software components while simultaneously developing a range of stand-alone applications—based on the business framework architecture—that can be marketed separately. Business framework is the new strategic R/3 product architecture. Integration technologies and open interfaces (BAPIs, i.e., object-oriented standard interfaces for integrating business applications) ensure interaction between these components and can integrate applications from third-party software providers, too.

—**Industry-specific solutions** SAP is strengthening its industry-specific activities. Prospective customers can select from a total of sixteen industry-specific solutions based on the SAP business framework.

—**New stand-alone business software products** SAP is introducing products based on the business framework architecture, i.e., advanced planner and optimizer, sales force automation, and business information warehouse.

1998: At the beginning of 1998, SAP's market capitalization increased to $38.5 billion, ranking it number three among German companies, behind Allianz and Deutsche Telekom. At the annual general meeting on May 7, 1988, cofounder Dietmar Hopp was elected chairman of the advisory board; Klaus Tschira was elected a member of the advisory board.

Appendix B:
On-line Sources

With kind permission of the moderators, the following references were partly gathered from the Frequently Asked Questions (FAQ) section of the Internet chat group news:de.alt.comp.sap-r3.

This source of information about SAP, published in English, is edited and updated by Andreas Bartelt in Oldenburg, Germany, in cooperation with Kaliana Kellye in Kalamazoo, Michigan.

Meanwhile, these answers to FAQ about SAP and its products are an important source of information and guidance for IT managers, SAP professionals, scientists, and students all around the world.

Comments, proposals, additions, and corrections can be sent to Andreas Bartelt at andreas.bartelt@informatik.uni-oldenburg or to Kaliana Kellye at connect@pro-connect.com.

The complete version contains, for example, addresses of many consulting firms, information about the SAP job market, and addresses of persons who are interested in SAP subjects. The SAP-FAQ can be retrieved with an Internet browser (e.g., Netscape Navigator or Microsoft Internet Explorer) at the following Web site: http://www.sapfaq.com.

SAP on the Internet

Individuals at SAP can be contacted by e-mail via the following model: firstname.lastname@sap-ag.de.

The magazine *SAP INFO* can be ordered by sending an e-mail to infoservice@sap-ag.de.

From the Internet there is no access to the internal communication network of SAP.

SAP's Web site can be found at http://www.sap.com.

CD-ROMs, information material, product booklets, product specifications, and customer information can be ordered at SAP via the Web at http://www.sap.com/shop.html.

Working Group "Universities"

The SAP Working Group "Universities" is financed by universities and SAP AG. Contact addresses are:

SAP-Arbeitskreis Hochschulen e.V.
SAP AG
Vorstand
D-69190 Walldorf
Germany

or

SAP-Arbeitskreis Hochschulen e.V.
c/o Prof. Dr. Oetinger
Goebenstraße 40
D-66117 Saarbrücken
Germany
Tel. +49-681-534 10
Fax +49-681-58 57 33

The Working Group "Universities" operates a Web site at the address http://vega.rz.uni-duesseldorf.de/-spiegl/SAP-AK/. Via e-mail you can reach the working group at sap-ak@uni-duesseldorf.de.

Mailing Lists

The e-mail list SAP-R3-L is dedicated to R/3 software. The contributions to discussions are automatically distributed via e-mail to all subscribers. The English language is used. Technical as well as nontechnical contributions are equally welcome. Advertising for products or services as well as commercial announcements are not allowed.

In order to get more information about the list, send your e-mail to listserv@mitvma.mit.edu with "INFO SAP-R3-L" as the first news line.

Newsgroups

Information exchange takes place in on-line newsgroups, too. Regularly or occasionally, SAP is the subject of discussions in the following newsgroups:

news:de.alt.comp.sap-r3
news:comp.client-server

Bibliography

AFOS. *SAP, Arbeit, Management—Durch systematische Gestaltung zum Projekterfolg*. Wiesbaden: Vieweg-Verlag, 1996.

Bancroft, Nancy. *Implementing SAP R/3: How to Introduce a Large System into a Large Organization*. Manning: 1996.

Barbitsch, C. *Einführung integrierter Standardsoftware—Handbuch für eine leistungsfähige Unternehmensorganisation*. München/Wien: Hanser-Verlag, 1996.

Bell, C. Gordon, with John E. McNamara. *High-Tech Ventures: The Guide for Entrepreneurial Success*. Reading: Addison-Wesley, 1991.

Brenner, W., and G. Keller. (Editors). *Business Reengineering mit Standardsoftware*. Frankfurt: Campus Verlag, 1995.

Buck-Emden, Rüdiger, and Jürgen Galimow. *Die Client Server-Technologie des Systems R/3*. Bonn: Addison-Wesley-Verlag, 1995.

CDI (Editor). *Praxistrainer SAP R/3 Einführung—Grundlagen, Anwendungen, Bedienung (für Release 3)*. Haar bei München: Markt & Technik Buch- und Software-Verlag, 1996.

Champy, James A. *Reengineering im Management. Die Radikalkur für die Unternehmensführung*. Frankfurt: Campus Verlag, 1995.

Christ, Angelika, and Steven Goldner. *Scientology im Management*. Düsseldorf: Econ-Verlag, 1996.

Coupland, Douglas. *Microsklaven*. Hamburg: Hoffmann und Campe-Verlag, 1996.

Davenport, Thomas H. *Process Innovation*. Boston: Harvard Business School Press, 1993.

Engels, A., J. Gresch, and M. Nottenkämper. *SAP R/3 kompakt—Einführung und Arbeitsbuch für die Praxis*. München: Tewi-Verlag, 1996.

Gassert, Herbert, and Manfred Prechtl. (Editors). *Neue Information-stechnologien. Bedeutung und Herausforderung für die Unternehmens-führung.* Stuttgart: Schäffler-Poeschel-Verlag, 1997.

Gates, Bill. *Der Weg nach vorn. Die Zukunft der Informationsge-sellschaft.* Hamburg: Hoffmann und Campe Verlag, 1995.

Gronau, Norbert. *Management von Produktion und Logistik mit SAP R/3.* München: Oldenbourg-Verlag, 1996.

Grupp, B. *EDV-Projekte in den Griff bekommen: Arbeitstechniken des Projektleiters; Planungs- und Überwachungsmethoden; Zusammenar-beit mit der Fachabteilung.* Köln: TÜV Rheinland, 1987.

Hammer, M., and J. Champy. *Business Reengineering. Die Radikalkur für das Unternehmen.* Frankfurt: Campus Verlag, 1994.

Hammer, Michael. "Reengineering Work: Don't Automate, Obliter-ate." *Harvard Business Review,* July–August 1990, pp. 104–12.

Keller, Gerhard, and Thomas Teufel. *SAP R/3 prozeßorientiert anwen-den.* Bonn: Addison-Wesley-Verlag, 1997.

Kirchner, M. *Geschäftsprozeßorientierte Einführung von Standardsoft-ware—Vorgehen zur Realisierung strategischer Ziele.* Wiesbaden: Gabler-Verlag, 1996.

Köglmayer, H.-G., and K. Porchert. "Festlegen und Ausführen von Geschäftsprozessen mit Hilfe von SAP-Software." *Beiträge aus dem Bericht der Wirtschaft Nr. 71,* FH Pforzheim, 1994.

Manes, Stephen, and Paul Andrews. *Gates. How Microsoft's Mogul Reinvented an Industry—and Made Himself the Richest Man in Amer-ica.* New York: Doubleday, 1993.

Martin, Hans-Peter, and Harald Schumacher. *Die Globalisierungsfalle. Der Angriff auf Demokratie und Wohlstand.* Reinbek bei Hamburg: Rowohlt-Verlag, 1996.

Negroponte, Nicholas. *Total digital. Die Welt zwischen 0 und 1 oder Die Zukunft der Komunikation.* München: C. Bertelsmann-Verlag, 1995.

Pack, Dr. Oskar. *25 schmutzige Tricks der Konkurrenz und wie Sie sich dagegen wehren.* Würzburg: Max Schimmel-Verlag, 1996.

Post, Henk A. *Ongoing Innovation: The Way We Built Baan.* Barneveld: Baan Business B. V., 1996.

Sampson, Anthony. *Die Manager. Portrait einer Führungskaste.* Hamburg: Hoffmann und Campe-Verlag, 1996.

Scheer, August-Wilhelm. *EDV-orientierte Betriebswirtschaftslehre.* Berlin: Springer-Verlag, 1990.

Scheer, August-Wilhelm. *Architektur integrierter Informationssysteme. Grundlagen der Unternehmensmodellierung.* Berlin: Springer-Verlag, 1992 (second edition).

Scheer, August-Wilhelm. *Wirtschaftsinformatik. Studienausgabe.* Berlin: Springer-Verlag, 1995.

Staute, Jörg. *Der Consulting-Report. Vom Versagen der Manager zum Reibach der Berater.* Frankfurt: Campus Verlag, 1996.

Thome, Rainer, and Andreas Hufgard. *Continuous System Engineering—Entdeckung der Standardsoftware als Organisator.* Würzburg: Vogel-Buchverlag, 1996.

Wallace, James, and Jim Erickson. *Mr. Microsoft. Die Bill Gates-Story.* Berlin: Ullstein-Verlag, 1993.

Wenzel, Paul (Editor). *Betriebswirtschaftliche Anwendungen des integrierten Systems SAP R/3: Projektstudien, Grundlagen und Anregungen für eine erfolgreiche Praxis.* Wiesbaden: Vieweg-Verlag, 1995.

Wenzel, Paul (Editor). *Geschäftsprozeßoptimierung mit SAP R/3: Modellierung, Steuerung und Management betriebswirtschaftlich-integrierter Geschäftsprozesse.* Wiesbaden: Vieweg-Verlag, 1995.

Whang, Sungjin, Wendell Gilland, and Hau Lee. *Information Flows in Manufacturing under SAP R/3. Case Study: Computer and Information Systems.* Stanford University Graduate School of Business, 1995.

SAP Addresses

SAP AG
Neurottstraße 16
61190 Walldorf
Germany
Tel. 49/62 27/7-47 474
Fax 49/62 27/7-57 575

AFRICA

SAPSA (Pty) Ltd.
SAP Business Park
1 Woodmead Drive
Woodmead 2148
P.O. Box 254
Randburg 2125
South Africa
Tel. 27/11/235-6000
Fax 27/11/235-6001

SAPSA (Pty) Ltd.
4th Floor, Morningside
Chambers
510, Windermere Road
Durban 4001
South Africa
Tel. 27/31/23-1157
Fax 27/31/23-2847

SAPSA (Pty) Ltd.
Metropolitan Life Building
25th Floor
7 Coen Steytler Avenue
Cape Town 8000
South Africa
Tel. 27/21/418-2860-7
Fax 7/21/419-9583

AMERICA

SAP America, Inc.
Strategic Planning & Support Office
3999 West Chester Pike
Newtown Square, PA 19073
Tel. 1 (610) 355-2500
Fax 1 (610) 355-3106

SAP America, Inc.
—Central Training
701 Lee Road
Wayne, PA 19087
Tel. 1 (610) 725-4317
Fax 1 (610) 725-4316

SAP America, Inc.
—FLCS
701 Lee Road
Wayne, PA 19087
Tel. 1 (610) 725-4545
Fax 1 (610) 725-4800

SAP America, Inc.
—Chicago
5 Westbrook Corporate Center
Suite 1000
Westchester, IL 60154
Tel. 1 (708) 947-3400
Fax 1 (708) 947-3404

SAP America, Inc.
—Cincinnati
312 Walnut Street
Suite 2470
Cincinnati, OH 45202
Tel. 1 (513) 977-5400
Fax 1 (513) 977-5401

SAP America, Inc.
—Cleveland
127 Public Square
Suite 5000
Cleveland, OH 44114
Tel. 1 (216) 615-3000
Fax 1(216) 615-3001

SAP America, Inc.
—Minneapolis
3530 Dain Rauscher Plaza
60 S. 6th Street
Minneapolis, MN 55402
Tel. 1 (612) 359-5000
Fax 1 (612) 359-5001

SAP America, Inc.
—St. Louis
City Place One
Suite 430
1 City Place
St. Louis, MO 63141
Tel. 1 (314) 213-7500
Fax 1 (314) 213-7501

SAP America, Inc.
—Boston
Bay Colony Corporate Center
950 Winter Street
Waltham, MA 02154
Tel. 1 (718) 672-6500
Fax 1 (718) 672-6501

SAP America, Inc.
—Parsippany
Morris Corporate Center
300 Interpace Parkway
Building A, 4th Floor
Parsippany, NJ 07054
Tel. 1 (973) 331-6000
Fax 1 (973) 331-6001

SAP America, Inc.
—Philadelphia
100 Stevens Drive
Philadelphia, PA 19113
Tel. 1 (610) 595-4900
Fax 1 (610) 521-6290

SAP America, Inc.
—Philadelphia (Data Center)
Two International Plaza
Suite 340
Philadelphia, PA 19113
Tel. 1 (610) 595-2400
Fax 1 (610) 521-2401

SAP America, Inc.
—Pittsburgh
301 Grant Street
One Oxford Center
Suite 1500
Pittsburgh, PA 15219-1417
Tel. 1 (412) 255-3795
Fax 1 (412) 255-3797

SAP America, Inc.
—Atlanta
Glenridge Highlands Ave.
555 Glenridge Connection
Atlanta, GA 30342
Tel. 1 (404) 943-2900
Fax 1 (404) 943-2950

SAP America, Inc.
—Houston
2500 City West Blvd.
Suite 1600
Houston, TX 77042
Tel. 1 (713) 917-5200
Fax 1 (713) 917-5201

SAP America, Inc.
—Dallas
600 East Las Colina Blvd.
Suite 2000
Irving, TX 75039
Tel. 1 (972) 868-2000
Fax 1 (972) 868-2001

SAP America, Inc.
—Seattle
800 Bellevue Way N.E.
4th Floor
Bellevue, WA 98004
Tel. 1 (425) 462-6395
Fax 1 (425) 462-2082

SAP America, Inc.
—Denver
4600 South Ulster Street
Suite 700
Denver, CO 80237
Tel. 1 (303) 740-6696
Fax 1 (303) 740-6612

SAP America, Inc.
—Foster City
950 Tower Lane
12th Floor
Foster City, CA 94404-2127
Tel. 1 (415) 637-1655
Fax 1 (415) 637-9592

SAP America, Inc.
—Irvine
18101 Von Karman Ave.
Suite 900
Irvine, CA 92612
Tel. 1 (949) 622-2200
Fax 1 (949) 622-2201

SAP America, Inc.
—Austin
Austin Center, Suite 800
701 Brazos
Austin, TX 78701
Tel. 1 (512) 425-2300
Fax 1 (512) 425-2301

SAP America, Inc.
—New York
One Liberty Plaza
165 Broadway, 51st Floor
New York, NY 10006
Tel. 1 (212) 346-5300
Fax 1 (212) 346-5301

SAP America, Inc.
—Miami
5201 Blue Lagoon Drive
Suite 580
Miami, FL 33126
Tel. 1 (305) 269-4300
Fax 1 (305) 269-4301

SAP America, Inc.
—Palo Alto
3475 Deer Creek Road
Palo Alto, CA 94304
Tel. 1 (650) 849-4000
Fax 1 (650) 849-4242

SAP America, Inc.
—Detroit
One Town Square
Suite 1550
Southfield, MI 48076
Tel. 1 (313) 304-1000
Fax 1 (313) 304-1001

SAP America, Inc.
—Public Sector
1300 Pennsylvania Ave, NW
Suite 500
Washington, D.C. 20004

SAP America, Inc.
—Americas Warehouse
496 Lapp Road
Malvern, PA 19355
Tel. 1 (610) 407-4269
Fax 1 (610) 407-9814

SAP Canada, Inc.
—Toronto
4120 Yonge Street
Suite 600
North York
Ontario M2P 2B8
Canada
Tel. 1 (416) 229-0574
Fax 1 (416) 229-0575

SAP Canada, Inc.
—Calgary
400 3rd Avenue, S.W.
Suite 600, Canterra Tower
Calgary, Alberta T2P 4H2
Canada
Tel. 1 (403) 269-5222
Fax 1 (403) 234-8082

SAP Canada, Inc.
—Montreal
380 Rue St. Antoine West
Suite 2000
Montreal, Quebec H2Y 3X7
Canada
Tel. 1 (514) 350-7300
Fax 1 (514) 350-7500

SAP Canada, Inc.
—Ottawa
45 O'Connor Street
Suite 600
Ottawa, Ontario K1P 1A4
Canada
Tel. 1 (613) 364-2500
Fax 1 (613) 364-2501

SAP Canada, Inc.
—Vancouver
666 Burrard Street
Suite 1550, Park Place
Vancouver
British Columbia V6C 2X8
Canada
Tel. 1 (604) 681-3809
Fax 1 (604) 688-0739

SAP Mexico S.A. DE C.V.
Edificio Plaza Reforma
Prolongación Paseo de la Reforma
    No 600-220
Piso Col. Peña Blanca Sta. Fé
C.P. 01210 México, D.F.
Mexico
Tel. 52/5/257-7500
Fax 52/5/257-7501

SAP Mexico S.A. DE C.V.
(Monterrey)
Av. Vasconcelos 101 Esq.
Rio Nazas
Edificio BBV 4to. Piso
66260 Garza Garcia, N.L.
Mexico
Tel. 52/8/152-1700
Fax 52/8/152-1701

SAP ARGENTINA S.A.
Torre Bouchard
Bouchard 547, 12° piso
1106 Buenos Aires
Argentina
Tel. 54/1/317-1700
Fax 54/1/317-1701

SAP Brasil Comércio
E Representações LTDA:
Av. das Nações Unidas,
11541—18° andar
Brooklin—São Paulo
SP 04578-000
Brazil
Tel. 55/11/532-2400
Fax 55/11/5505-2307

SAP Brasil
—Porto Alegre
Av. Calos Gomes, 328 cj.
707/708
Porto Alegre—RS
CEP: 90480-000
Brazil
Tel. 55/51/328-6401
Fax 55/51/328-6401

SAP Brasil
—Ribeirão Preto
Av. Portugal, 1740—sala 31
Ribeirão Preto—SP
CEP: 14020-380
Brazil
Tel. 55/16/620-1284
Fax 55/16/620-1294

SAP Agencia En Chile
Av. Apoquindo 4499, piso 12
Las Condes
Santiago de Chile
Chile
Tel. 56/2/440-3500
Fax 56/2/440-3501

SAP Colombia

Calle 114 # 9-45
Teleport Business Park
Tower B, 14th Floor
Santafe de Bogotá
Colombia
Tel. 57/1/629-4930
Fax 57/1/629-4486

SAP Andina y del
Caribe C.A.

Avenida Principal de la Castellana
Torre ING Bank, Centro Letonia
Piso 13
La Castellana 1060
Venezuela
Tel. 58/2/267-5400
Fax 58/2/267-4327

SAP Peru

Calle San Ignacio de Loyoala No. 554
Miraflores
Lima 18
Peru
Tel. 51/1/242-1215

AUSTRALASIA

SAP Australia Pty Ltd

Level 1
Northside Gardens
168 Walker Street
North Sydney, NSW 2060
Australia
Tel. 61/2/99 35-4500
Fax 61/2/99 35-4644

SAP Australia Pty Ltd

Level 24
State Bank Building
91 King William Street
Adelaide, SA 5000
Australia
Tel. 61/8/233-5814
Fax 61/8/233-5834

SAP Australia Pty Ltd

Level 12
133 Mary Street
Brisbane, QLD 4000
Australia
Tel. 61/7/32 59-9500
Fax 61/7/32 59-9599

SAP Australia Pty Ltd

Level 2, Digital Building
564 St. Kilda Road
Melbourne, VIC 3004
Australia
Tel. 61/3/92 07-4100
Fax 61/3/92 07-4244

SAP Australia Pty Ltd

Level 18, Central Park
152-158 St. George's Terrace
Perth, WA 6000
Australia
Tel. 61/9/288-4505
Fax 61/9/288-4504

SAP Australia Pty Ltd
SATirnt College
910 Pacific Highway
Gordon, NSW 2072
Australia
Tel. 61/2/9935-4510
Fax 61/2/99 35-4520

SAP Australia Pty Ltd
Level 12, Canberra Centre Tower
Akuna & Bunda Streets
Canberra, ACT 2601
Australia
Tel. 61/2/62 14-0300
Fax 61/2/62 14-0399

SAP New Zealand Limited
Level 10, Microsoft House
67-69 Symonds Street
Auckland, New Zealand
Tel. 64/9/355-6800
Fax 64/9/355-5890

SAP New Zealand Limited
Level 5, Castrol House
36 Customhouse Quay
Wellington, New Zealand
Tel. 64/4/499-9866
Fax 64/4/499-8035

ASIA

SAP Asia Pte. Ltd.
750A Chai Chee Road
7th Floor Chai Chee
Industrial Park
Singapore 469001
Tel. 65/446-1800
Fax 65/249-1818

SAP Asia Pte. Ltd.
83 Clemenceau Avenue
17-01 UE Square
Singapore 23 99 20
Tel. 65/738-2688
Fax 65/249-1838

SAP (Beijing) Software System Co., Ltd.
99 Shuang Qing Lu
Hai Dian District
Beijing 100084, China
Tel. 86/10/6262-3388
Fax 86/10/6261-0204

SAP Shanghai Office
Shanghai Royal Court
No. 7, Lane 622
Huai Hai Road Middle
Shanghai 200020, China
Tel. 86/21/63 58-3388
Fax 86/21/63 58-1818

SAP Hong Kong
Suite 1111-1114, 11/F
Cityplaza 4
12 Taikoo Wan Road
Taikoo Shing, Hong Kong
Tel. 852/25 39-1800
Fax 852/25 39-1818

SAP India Pvt. Ltd.
Thapar Niketan
2nd & 3rd Floor
Brunton Road
Bangalore 560025
India
Tel. 91/80/509-5056
Fax 91/80/509-5055

SAP India Pvt. Ltd.
c/o Consultair
Investments Pvt. Ltd.
Khetan Bhavan
5th Floor
198, J Tata Road
Bombay 400 020
India
Tel. 91/22/28 26824
Fax 91/22/28 83796

SAP Indonesia
Wisma Kyoei Prince
1928 Lalan Jenderal
Sudirman Kav 3
Jakarta 10220
Indonesia
Tel. 62/21/572-4289
Fax 62/21/572-4292

SAP Japan Co., Ltd.
TIME 24 Bldg. 7th Floor
2-45 Aomi, Koto-ku
Tokyo 135-8073
Japan
Tel. 81/3/55 31-3333
Fax 81/3/55 31-1011

SAP Japan Co., Ltd.
Kobe Chrystal Tower
18th Floor
1-1-3 Higashi
Kawasaki-cho
Chuo-ku, Kobe 650-0044
Japan
Tel. 81/78/362-7880
Fax 81/78/362-7881

SAP Japan Co., Ltd.
Aishin Chiyomi Bldg.
10th Floor
1-100 Chiyomi
Tottori, 680-0911
Japan
Tel. 81/857/37-1950
Fax 81/857/37-1979

SAP Korea Limited
23/F Ssang Yong Tower
23-2 Yoido-dong
Youngdeungpo-ku
Seoul 150-010
Korea
Tel. 82/2/37 71-1810
Fax 82/2/37 71-1818

**SAP Data Processing
(Malaysia) Sdn Bhd**
12th Floor, Menara
Tan & Tan
207 Jalan Tun Razak
50200 Kuala Lumpur
Malaysia
Tel. 60/3/261-0233
Fax 60/3/261-2688

SAP Philippines, Inc.
32/F Citibank Tower
Citibank Plaza
8741 Paseo de Roxas
Makati City, Metro Manila
Philippines
Tel. 63/2/848-0181
Fax 63/2/848-0168

SAP Taiwan Co. Ltd.
18F Suite
No. 156 Min Sheng E.
Road Sec. 3
Taipei, Taiwan
Tel. 886/2/25 46-1800
Fax 886/2/25 14-6418

SAP Thailand Ltd
287 Liberty Square
22nd Floor
Silom Road
Bangkok 10500
Thailand
Tel. 66/2/631-1800
Fax 66/2/631-1819

EUROPE

N.V. SAP Belgium S.A.
2, Boulevard de la
Woluwé
1150 Bruxelles
Belgium
Tel. 32/2/778-5011
Fax 32/2/772-5051

SAP AG
Representative Office
Michailovskaya 8A
252001 Kiev
Ukraine
Tel. 38/044/247-7040
Fax 38/044/247-7041

SAP AG
Representative Office
Kosmodamianskaya nab. 52/2
113054 Moscow
Russia
Tel. 7/095/755-9800
Fax 7/095/755-9801

SAP AG
Representative Office
Dostyk, 43
480100 Almaty
Kazakhstan
Tel. 7/33 72/54 0110
Fax 7/33 72/54 0120

000 SAP Consult
Simonovski Val, D. 26a
113054 Moscow
Russia
Tel. 7/095/275-0454
Fax 7/095/956-9325

SAP CR, s.r.o.
K Hajum 948
155 00 Prague 5
Czech Republic
Tel. 42/02/65 197-01
Fax 42/02/65 198-43

SAP AG
Representative Office
ABACUS House
House 13
Line 4, V.O.
St. Petersburg
Russia

SAP CR, s.r.o.
Junacke 1077
70200 Ostrava—Stara
Bela
Czech Republic
Tel. 42/069/67 207-00
Fax 42/069/67 207-10

SAP CR, s.r.o.
Videnska 55
63999 Brno
Czech Republic
Tel. 42/05/43 52 43-01
Fax 42/05/43 52 43-13

SAP CR, s.r.o.
—org.zlozka
Kutlikova 17
P.O. Box 229
85000 Bratislava 5
Slovak Republic
Tel. 42/17/834-663
Fax 42/17/830-792

SAP Danmark A/S
Ringager 48
2605 BrØndby/Copenhagen
Denmark
Tel. 45/43 26-3900
Fax 45/43 26-3901

SAP Espana y
Portugal S.A.
Edificio Torre Picasso
Plaza Pablo Ruiz Picasso
Planta 4
28020 Madrid
Spain
Tel. 34/1/456-7200
Fax 34/1/456-7201

SAP Espana y
Portugal S.A.
Edificio Torre Mapfre
Carrer de la Marina 16-18
Planta 11
08005 Barcelona
Spain
Tel. 34/3/483-3500
Fax 34/3/483-3501

SAP Espana y
Portugal S.A.
Edificio Restelo
Rua D. Cristovao da Gama
1-2° A B
1400 Lisbon
Portugal
Tel. 351/1/303-0300
Fax 351/1/303-0301

SAP Finland
Valkjärventie 2
02130 Espoo
Finland
Tel. 358/9/61 33 3-030
Fax 358/9/61 33 3-099

SAP France S.A.
Head Office
57-59, Boulevard
Malesherbes
75008 Paris
France
Tel. 33/1/55 30-2000
Fax 33/1/55 30-2001

SAP France S.A.
Training and R/3 University
"Les Olympiades"
10/12 Avenue des
Olympiades
94132 Fontenay-sous-Bois
France
Tel. 33/1/49 74-4545
Fax 33/1/48 75-5266

SAP Italia S.p.A.
Centro Direzionale
Viale Colleoni 17
Palazzo Orione 3
20041 Agrate
Brianza/Milano
Italy
Tel. 39/39/6879-1
Fax 39/39/6091-005

SAP Italia S.p.A.
Via Mario Bianchini 51
00142 Roma
Italy
Tel. 39/6/51 956-122
Fax 39/6/51 956-127

**SAP Service & Support
Centre (Ireland) Ltd.**
Eastpoint Business Park
Fairview
Dublin 3,
Ireland
Tel. 353/1/855-8854
Fax 353/1/855-2884

SAP Luxembourg S.A.
3A, Rue Guillaume Kroll
1882 Luxembourg
Luxembourg
Tel. 352/49/000-6210
Fax 352/49/000-6635

SAP Nederland B.V.
Bruistensingel 400
5203 AG
's-Hertogenbosch
Netherlands
Tel. 31/73/645-7526
Fax 31/73/641-9130

SAP Norge A/S
Vollsveien 6
1324 Lysaker
Norway
Tel. 47/67/529-400
Fax 47/67/529-401

**SAP Österreich GmbH
—Wien**
Stadlauer Str. 54
Postfach 25
1221 Vienna
Austria
Tel. 43/1/288-220
Fax 43/1/288-22222

SAP Österreich GmbH
Langgasse 11
4020 Linz
Austria
Tel. 43/732/60 04 60-0
Fax 43/732/60 04 60-11

SAP Österreich GmbH
Loiger Strasse 220
5071 Salzburg-Wals
Austria
Tel. 43/662/853-687
Fax 43/662/853-68722

**SAP Österreich GmbH
—Budapest Kereskedelmi**
Képviseleti Iroda
Magyarország
H-1122 Budapest
Városmajor u. 13
Leveélcim: H-1535
Budapest PF.931
Hungary
Tel. 36/1/457-8333
Fax 36/1/457-8344

**SAP Hungary
Renszerek,
Alkalmazások és
Termékek az
Adatfeldolgozásban
Informatikai Kft.**
H-1122 Budapest
Városmajor u. 13
Hungary
Tel. 36/1/457-8333
Fax 36/1/457-8344

SAP Polska Sp. z.o.o.
Mokotow Business Park
ul. Domaniewska 41/16A
02672 Warsaw
Poland
Tel. 48/22/60 60-606
Fax 48/22/60 60-607

SAP Svenska AB
Gustavslundvägen 151 B
10227 Stockholm
Sweden
Tel. 46/8/80-9680
Fax 46/8/26-2278

SAP (Schweiz) AG
Postfach 130
Leugenestrasse 6
2500 Biel 6
Switzerland
Tel. 41/32/34 47-111
Fax 41/32/34 47-211

SAP (Schweiz) AG
Training Centre (Zürich)
Eichwatt 3
8105 Regensdorf
Switzerland
Tel. 41/1/87 11-511
Fax 41/1/84 10-708

SAP (Suisse) SA
WTCL
Avenue Gratta-Paille 2
Case postale 469
1000 Lausanne 30 Grey
Switzerland
Tel. 41/21/641-5555
Fax 41/21/641-5550

SAP (UK) Limited
Clockhouse Place
Bedfont Road
Feltham
Middlesex, TW14 8HD
United Kingdom
Tel. 44/870/608-4000
Fax 44/870/608-4050

SAP (UK) Ltd
Training Centre
1, Nobel Drive
Hayes
Feltham
Middlesex, UB3 5EY
United Kingdom
Tel. 44/181/818-2991/2
Fax 44/181/844-0876

SALES PARTNERS

Advanced Technology Ltd.
Atidim Neve Sharet
P.O. Box 58 180
Tel Aviv 61 581
Israel
Tel. 972/3/54 83-530
Fax 972/3/54 83-653

SAP Arabia
1st. Fl. Enany
Headquarters Bldg.
Al-Malek Road (beside
    Leylaty Bldg.)
Jeddah 21 493
Saudi Arabia
Tel. 966/2/66 22-217
Fax 966/2/69 14-114

SAP Arabia
P.O. Box 53 188
Dubai
City Tower 1, Suite 1009
U.A.E. Shk. Zayed Road
United Arab Emirates
Tel. 971/4 31-0777
Fax 971/4 31-0410

SAP Bilgi Islem Sistemleri ve Servisleri A.S.
Fahtettin Kerim Goekay
Cad. No. 22
81190 Altunizade/Istanbul
Turkey
Tel. 90/216/391-8462
Fax 902/216/391-4555

SAP Hellas S.A.
103 Kallioris Street
17671 Athens
Greece
Tel. 301/924-0242
Fax 301/924-0350

SAP Hrvatska, d.o.o. za informacijska rjesenja
Savska 41
10000 Zagreb
Croatia
Tel. 385/1/61 21-460
Fax 385/1/61 19-016

SAP (Cyprus) Ltd.
12 Grigori Afxentiou
2360 Ayios Dhometios
1703 Nicosia
Cyprus
Tel. 357/2/780-086
Fax 357/2/780-089

SAP Romania SRL
21, Calea Victorei
etaj VI-VII
Bucharest –3
Romania
Tel. 40/1/312-5929
Fax 40/1/312-4138

SEITZ Information Systems
59, Solunska Str.
1000 Sofia
Bulgaria
Tel. 359/2/95 15-478
Fax 359/2/95 15-875

Probis d.o.o.
Slandrova ul. 2
1231 Llubljana-Crnuce
Slovenia
Tel. 386/61/18 95-400
Fax 386/61/18 95-401

Index